Speak the Word

Expect the Wonder

Discovering the Power and
Passion of the Word

To a new friend
in Christ,

Bro. Henson

Dr. Ernest R. Henson

Chairman, Missions Dept, NorthPoint Bible College

Speak the Word, Expect the Wonder
By Ernest R. Henson

Published by Fire & Rain Publishing LLC, Haverhill, MA

ISBN 978-0-9830920-1-8

Contents

ACKNOWLEDGMENTS

This writer is thankful for my wife, Linda. Almost all the narrative sections of these nine chapters have involved her participation and gracious assistance. I stand in amazement at her constancy and love for these almost fifty years together. Her encouraging and insightful words have sustained me throughout both the living and writing of this volume. After my gratitude to the Lord I mostly thank her for always being there to keep me focused. I also praise God for our two daughters Angela and Ami who have lived through many of the accounts told in this book whether they were aware of events at the time of their occurrence or not. I am grateful for our four grandchildren, Jared, Ashley, Austin and Judson who will, I believe, carry out the spiritual legacy begun in the telling of the stories within its pages.

I express a big thank you to Dr. Bonnie Boyington for her diligence in taking on the arduous task of editing this writing. I know it had to be the sustaining power of the Holy Spirit that gave her the grace to finish the work. I also wish to thank my pastor and friend, Rev. Wayne L. Shirk for his counsel and encouragement. I want to acknowledge my appreciation to the Administration of North Point Bible College for giving me the opportunity of teaching in such a great school. Finally, thank you to all my students who have allowed my wife and I the privilege of 'hanging out' with you and for the experience of sharing a bit of our lives with you.

PREFACE

This book's purpose is singular in that it has been written to emphasize the force of God's Word to impact humanity. It also has a focus that is two-fold. One focus is to encourage all believers to keep before them the divine energy that is released when verbally sharing the Word of God and what it has wrought within them by its transforming power. The Word of God is His "good seed" (Lk. 8:11), and therefore wherever it is sown it has the potential to produce spiritual transformation and supernatural manifestation (Mk. 1:21-26). The Word of God supernaturally impacts people as it is witnessed to by any and all believers. My calling through these pages is to simply keep believers reminded of the wonderful dynamic we all have available to us in the Word of God when it is verbally communicated.

A second focus of this volume is to particularly challenge those who carry the weekly human privilege and divine burden of preaching and teaching the Word of God vocationally. This writing attempts to remind preachers of the importance of maintaining a sense of expectancy as they preach and teach God's Word.

Also, we who are called to such a blessing have the responsibility of promoting that same sense of expectancy within the hearts and minds of those to whom we preach. The intentional attitude that I am attempting to encourage through this research is what I call *faith expectation.* It is this mindset that is most conducive to the Church's experiencing a greater revival of Kingdom reality for an end-time explosion of global harvest. This writer makes no claim to having achieved this biblical vision for witness and ministry. It is a life-long goal to which I aspire and is a *faith expectation* I will pursue until faith becomes reality. In the words of the Apostle Paul "Not that I have already attained, or am already perfected; but I press on, that I may lay hold of that for which Christ Jesus has also laid hold of me" (Phil. 3:12). For the moment this desire and longing still lies within the realm of hope and anticipation (Heb. 11:1). I believe, however, that this attitude of expectancy will help to usher in the restored New Testament pattern for witness in general and preaching in particular. This atmosphere, in turn, will initiate the greatest evangelistic harvest and missionary outreach this earth has ever seen. As Jesus Himself, declared: "And this Gospel of the kingdom will be preached in all the world as a witness to all the nations, and then the end will come" (Mt. 24:14). Therefore, by all means possible and every moment left, let us *Speak the Word, Expect the Wonder!*

INTRODUCTION

What? Another book about preaching! Yes, it is another book on preaching, but it is addressed not just to those who preach as part of their professional calling, but to all believers who bear witness to the Word of God no matter what their vocational or professional capacity might be. Therefore, this text is written to and for anyone who dares to embrace the awesome privilege of declaring the powerful words of Scripture with the empowering of the Holy Spirit.

It is, therefore, not a book on methods, types, styles or even developmental content for sermon preparation and delivery. All of the hermeneutical tools and techniques of preaching related to exegesis, exposition and application are readily available to anyone who wants to acquire greater skills in these areas. Most preachers have already been equipped with how to prepare and preach sermons in Bible college, seminary or by reading the many excellent volumes of homiletics already available to the public.

Almost anyone who aspires to speaking or witnessing to God's Word can accumulate sufficient information and knowledge from books on preaching methods, witnessing tools or communication theory. I am personally aware of multiple resources since I have read, taught and done research from many of those volumes. During my decades of preaching I have collected and have been thoroughly blessed and challenged by many volumes on the art and science of communication. There are already many preachers, practitioners, and professors who can teach and model principles and practices of proclaiming God's Word.

The value of this volume and of my contribution to the act of preaching lies rather in my singular focus of speaking and bearing witness to the Word for supernatural results. There are others who have pioneered this approach, but I believe my fifty-four years of preaching experience might add a few significant and challenging insights.

Although much of this book's content is about the importance of supernatural signs and wonders, its all-embracing focus is about preaching. Everything that is written about the value of the miraculous dimension is related to the impact that is generated by, and the power that comes through, proclamation of the Gospel. I acknowledge that miracles are complimentary to, and even an essential ingredient of preaching but they are not equal in purpose to preaching or speaking the Gospel. Miracles should be seen as either the outflow of preaching or as the invitational platform for preaching. Viewed from the perspective of a public drama, proclamation of the Word plays the leading role in God's divine production, whereas, miracles represent the important supporting cast. As I read Scripture, Jesus always moved about preaching and teaching and miracles just seemed to follow as a normal course of action. When Jesus sent the disciples out to witness, they went about preaching and teaching; signs and wonders occurred as a natural response to the spiritual force of the message they proclaimed. Proclamation and bearing witness to the Gospel was the supernatural cause; wonders were the supernatural effect.

I take my cue for this natural procedure from Jesus where He said to His disciples, "Let us go into the next towns that I may preach there also, because for this purpose I have come forth" (Mark 1:38). The following verses in that chapter describe some power-encounters that took place after He preached as a natural occurrence. Then in relation to Jesus calling the twelve disciples, the Gospel writer says "He appointed twelve that they might be with Him and that He might send them out to preach" (Mark 3:14). The following verse then acknowledges that they also had the "power to heal sicknesses and to cast out demons" (Mark 3:15). All the other Gospels seem to indicate that the Gospel priority is always that of proclamation, but wherever there was witnessing to the Word, power was always released for the miraculous to take place. There is much more that could and will be said about the relationship between preaching and miracles, but the connection is essentially one of cause and effect. This design pattern is the biblical norm.

My years of preaching and teaching have only served to reinforce my confidence in the proclaimed Word, not because my speaking has ever measured up to that biblical norm, but because of the firm belief that we should never settle for less than the Scriptural ideal. I also press toward this biblical norm because I believe it is God's weapon of choice for the Church's effectiveness during the Church age. It is my conviction that a true restoration of New Testament preaching and speaking the Word will be the Spirit's instrument of ushering in an end-time revival that will confirm the true nature and power of God's Word. I contend that it is the event of proclaiming the supernatural Gospel of Christ under the empowered anointing of the Spirit that will convict the animist, confound the atheist and even convince the radical terrorist. Only the proclamation of this kind of Spirit-empowered Gospel will have this kind of impact on the rampaging forces of the enemy arrayed against us.

I warn the perspective reader that this book will share one thing in common with all the other literature on homiletics he or she has ever read: It deliberately sends out the relentless trumpet call "to preach the Word" (2 Tim. 4:2). I know that this admonition can become a catch phrase to receive quick applause, a positive response or the thunderous roar of a pious "amen". I also readily affirm that this phrase "to preach the Word" truly expresses what is most hallowed to our calling. Unfortunately, I fear that I have too often used the phrase as a self-righteous cover-up for having missed Paul's admonishing challenge so badly. My personal concern is that if I had truly been faithful "to preach the Word" the results would not have been so paltry. The apostle's exhortation "to preach the Word" is still a time honored and hallowed ambition to all believers. However, I hope that reading this book will give new meaning to that high calling and a fresh sense of the human impossibility of accomplishing its full potential, without the Holy Spirit's complete enabling.

If there is one primary difference between this book and most other volumes on preaching, it is the single goal and persistent challenge to the reader to acquire a sense of faith expectancy when proclaiming the Word of God. I encourage the development of a divine discontent, not so much toward the content preached, or with any particular style of preaching, but with proclamation that produces inadequate supernatural results. We must not discredit any good supernatural seed, but we must inspect the fruit of our proclamation with greater discernment and discretion. When I use the phrase "to preach the Word", I now remind myself of Jesus' supernatural results when He preached the Word. After such reflection, I am no longer as self-assured as I used to be that I have really been preaching the Word.

Now, when I try to encourage others about the function of preaching, I am able to reject any sense of arrogance or boasting because my mental model is that of Jesus. I don't feel as inadequate so long as I compare my preaching with human norms and westernized expectations, but when I compare my preaching with the apostles and the early believers, I realize just how far I have yet to go. When they went out to "preach the Word," miracles happened; lives were radically changed by the thousands and people were set free of all of Satan's oppressions. These supernatural effects were common, not just for the apostles who preached, but for Spirit-filled believers who simply went out bearing witness to the Word.

In retrospect I now cringe when I think about how I have used that phrase even while I was making the Word as dry as sawdust. I have been guilty of mimicking the challenge "to preach the Word" and using it as a reference for just quoting supporting scriptures or for rigidly adhering to the rules of exegeting every nuance of the text. The phrase can also reflect a forced coherence to either the traditional word by word exposition or even the legalistic following of the hermeneutical spiral. Of course, those methods are all good so long as we don't intellectualize the life out of the text. It is good to keep in mind that if the Spirit gives us the text to preach, that text is already alive and by the Spirit's anointing it will become rationally relevant and spiritually vibrant. We can have the greatest of confidence that the Word of God is a living reality and will do its work. The Words of Christ have the innate energy to produce the Spirit's manifestations. Our biggest task is to make sure we don't diminish its vitality with our own low expectations. The Word and Spirit will do their part when we maintain the proper attitude of faith expectancy. It is this writer's opinion that preaching is most often ineffective, not because we have given too little time to sermon preparation, but because we have given too little time to self-preparation. It is best to give adequate time to allow the Spirit to build up our confidence in the power of the Word in order to affect the Spirit's intended outcome.

I believe that God has given us the solution for reinvigorating the Church and reaching our contemporary world through none other than the event of preaching and witnessing to His Word. However, our delivery must be by proclamation that reflects, not "the letter of the law" but rather "the life of the Spirit" (Rom.7:6). It must be the type of verbal communication that truly holds out to the world the promise that the Gospel really is Good News, that it has the power to change us and to alter situations and restore divine blessings to every dimension of human existence. It is preaching that delivers the challenge to trust God's Word to meet needs, heal bodies, deliver from addictions, cast out demons and liberate people from whatever is oppressing them.

My admonition, therefore, is quite simple and is suggested by my title "to speak the Word" and expect the wonder! Yes, the focused challenge is "to preach the Word" for the power of Christ is contained within His Gospel, His message, His truth, His Word. According to Scripture, when His message is proclaimed, there should be a corresponding expectation on our part. Every appropriation of divine grace anticipates a reciprocal response of human faith. It is the interaction of the unmerited favor of Christ with our intentional response of faith that activates the Spirit's supernatural effects or miraculous demonstrations. What is the problem then? Where might the difficulty lie? I believe the answer is obvious. The fault lies not with God's grace, so that must mean that the area of difficulty lies with our response.

Of course, in order for supernatural things to happen, it must be the action and the will of the Spirit. However, there is one human attitude that God's preachers and God's witnesses must appropriate to a greater degree to best facilitate the Spirit's initiative. That attitude is one that genuinely anticipates divine response and Spirit-given manifestation. I believe Jesus' word for that kind of anticipatory mind-set and sense of absolute expectancy was called faith (Lk. 7:9; 17:19). The absence of this confidence in God and His Word is about the only reaction that limits His will to act on our behalf (Mt. 13:56). Faith is a wonderful word, but because of all the baggage it has been forced to bear, I believe the word "expectation" conveys the message very adequately. For God to act most decisively, we as Christ's Church need to develop a fresh response of confident expectation when it comes to the witness of God's Word. Christ's preachers and saints alike need to reenergize their faith in the Word when it is declared, not because of the one doing the speaking, but because of the power in the message being preached.

My hope for anyone who reads this volume is that he or she will be reinvigorated to trust the Word to do its work and produce

God's mighty wonders in the midst of the Church in such a way as to impact the world. Pastors, begin to anticipate that people in your congregations will be healed during the service or receive their miracle during the week as a direct result of the proclaimed Word. Ask the Spirit to renew your own sense of expectation in connection to the preaching of the Word as you believe for the mighty acts of God. Let God's people know that you are really anticipating their needs to be met; spiritually, emotionally, relationally and physically during your ministering of God's powerful and dynamic Word. May it never be said of us as was said of unbelieving Israel: "For indeed the gospel was preached to us as well as to them; but the word which they heard did not profit them, not being mixed with faith in those who heard it" (Heb. 4:2). This kind of faith or expectancy need be neither whimsically feeble nor demandingly brash. According to the book of Hebrews, true faith neither attempts to work anything up nor does it frantically fret, but simply enters into a confident mode of relaxing in the Lord (4:9-12). The single repeated word is *Expect! Expect! Expect!* Expectation is simply our response of faith to Christ's initiative of grace.

Finally, my desire for you, the reader, is that during your reading of this volume you will experience both moments of laughter and of weeping. I wish upon you laughter, not because I am such a humorous writer or because this content is such funny material, but that you will experience the deeper joy that comes from what the Spirit alone can prompt. I am speaking about that deep joy that comes when "deep calls unto deep" (Ps. 42:7), or when the unlimited depth of the Spirit speaks to the limited depth of your spirit and you know that you have been invited into His inner chamber of healing communion and powerful presence.

Also, I desire that this read will even produce some moments of brokenness, not because I want to cause pain, or because I think that you are in need of some emotional catharsis, but because sometimes that's the way the Spirit chooses to initiate greater healing and empowerment. When our tears are truly of the Spirit, they become the reenactment of His tears. They allow us to feel a little more deeply what He felt in His ministry on His way to the cross. But, while none of us will have to experience the full violence of the cross, all believers that dare to minister His Word get to experience the partial pain of Gethsemane.

So, there you have it! I have just given to you my understanding of what the essence of bearing forth the Word really is. It is our privilege and responsibility to participate in both the sufferings and the glory of Christ. It is the believer's invitation to experience both the depth of God's revealed message and the height of His miraculous wonders. Therefore, SPEAK THE WORD AND EXPECT THE WONDER!

CHAPTER ONE

1 CORINTHIANS 1: 19-31

PREACHING; ALTERNATIVE TO PERISHING

A NARRATIVE RESPONSE TO THE TEXT

It was a hot summer morning in July of 1952. Sitting on a well-worn and sticky pew in the sweltering heat of an older frame church at Camp Cottonwood, an eleven year old boy had his first encounter with the Word of God preached. I was that young lad forever changed by the convicting power of preaching. There were many other external influencing factors that led to my conversion, but it was the personal encounter with the Word of God that grasped my youthful attention and launched my life-long commitment to Christ. However, like all testimonies, the story begins earlier.

Even as a young boy without a lot of early involvement in church, I acquired an unconscious attraction to the art of preaching. Before I was nine years old I had little to do with church except for an occasional forced Sunday school attendance at a nearby Free Methodist Church where my Aunt Evelyn was a faithful member and my Uncle Tony often preached. I definitely did not care for church; it was too much of a distraction to my boyish sense of adventure and worldly intrigue. Yet, I was fascinated at the emotive and passionate preaching of Uncle Tony when family loyalty forced me to stay for morning worship. Curiously, my outward reluctance did not obscure my inward longing to know more about why one could get so animated about any subject. Even my lack of parental guidance and encouragement toward spiritual matters could not obliterate my deep attraction to the exuberant style of the preacher or the engaging content of his message.

Perhaps what was also unconsciously alluring was my consistently hearing the lilting sounds of melodious music and vibrant preaching every summer from old Camp Beulah no more than six blocks from my home. In southern Illinois, Camp Beulah was known for being the old time Holiness camp grounds and had maintained a widespread image of fiery revival from a Wesleyan tradition. For many Holiness people it was hallowed ground and a place where many a soul could lay claim to the immediate experience of sanctification. The physical energy and emotional vibrations of the preaching and worship were often carried along by the hot summer and evening air. Even the recollection of these long past mental images are still grooved into my memory, some sixty-five years later. To this day, I can still feel the impact of the distant and lingering sound-waves of those long forgotten camp meetings.

At the age of nine my family moved out to the country where my mother started taking my three brothers and me to the rural Baptist Church a few miles from where we had moved. It wasn't long until I saw first hand the impact of forceful and convicting preaching. I sat in a back pew with bewilderment and amazement as I saw my mother respond to the altar call for sinners to be converted. I saw and came to more fully understand the power of preaching that day and its ability to draw the human spirit into the miracle of new birth. Beginning that Sunday morning, I saw my mother become a new and changed person before my young and dubious eyes. I saw a woman hardened by years of verbal abuse, emotional neglect and loss of two children turned into a faithful and loving Christian woman and mother, softened by the touch of the Spirit's regenerating embrace. That good seed of the Word of God that was sown in the soil of her heart that day continued to grow and produce the fruits of righteousness until the Lord of the Harvest took her home at the age of ninety-six. Until the day of her very last breath, she was devoted to both the written Word which sustained her and to the preached Word that had rescued her from her anxious and resentful past.

From the day I observed my mother's new life-change, I began to pay even closer attention to the preachers as they proclaimed the Bible stories and messages with powerful force and passionate persuasion. I came to admire those early pastor-preachers because they always shed such depth of insight and understanding on the Scriptures. Yet, those preachers that nurtured and informed my earliest training had little or no theological education or academic background. Most of them barely had an elementary education, but to a person they preached with revelatory illumination and prophetic conviction. I'm sure that none of them consciously performed the hermeneutical exercises and exegetical requirements as taught and demanded in the classrooms of academia. However, I believe they had their own Spirit-directed form of exegesis, exposition and application that expressed no lack of content or no crisis of relevance in their homiletic style. When it came to preaching for repentance, holy living and Holy Spirit-encounter, they were effective ministers of the Word.

An emotional draw to preaching continued in my youthful consciousness and throughout my early years, but preaching's true existential impact upon my own life was yet to unfold, along with my own conversion narrative. It was there in that small church sanctuary at Camp Cottonwood on that July morning, I became entranced seeing a boy my own age introduced who then started preaching the morning message. Neither heat, humidity, regimented camp life, nor mild homesickness could distract my attention from the conviction of my lost state before the God of heaven as that twelve year old boy preached his sermon. I was shocked that someone my age was preaching, but I was also amazed that his words carried the same convincing force as had the words of all the other preachers I had ever heard. It would not be until the evening service that my reluctance would be fully overcome as I was drawn by the Spirit to the church altar, but I knew it had been the anointed message of that young preacher that made my repentance and faith a fore-drawn conclusion.

As one can see, even my early life was a subtle romance with the art of proclaiming the Gospel. One could say that my life has held a lifelong fascination with it. I have had a growing sense of preaching's place and importance in the over-all scheme of my life, thought and ministry. It is not my intention to discredit or diminish the myriad aspects of ministry, but my years in ministry have simply reinforced the belief that proclamation of, or witness to the Gospel, is the pinnacle of our calling. It would be another four years before I would consciously recognize my own teenage call into the journey of the preaching ministry. However, even those seeming insignificant years would only continue to inflame a consciousness of God and ignite a passion for bearing witness to His Word.

From the age of eleven to fifteen, my years held times of typical teenage struggling, along with adolescent growth and compromise, but they were also years of increasing appreciation and awe of the preached and spoken Word. During those years my family moved several times, but we were able to maintain some sporadic involvement with our home church. At the age of fifteen the formational and transformational force of the Word of God began to have an effect upon my own spiritual development. I maintained an ever growing desire to discover for myself the internal and artesian source of those who stood up to preach the Gospel. It was the mystery of preaching that led me to search out for myself the unfathomable wisdom within the Bible. The more I read its pages, the more I became enamored at this Book's ability to reveal its insights even to my teenage mind. The hunger for biblical knowledge became insatiable. I could not refrain from reading the Bible; it had truly become for me God's own Word of direction, development and deliverance.

During my last years of High School I read the Bible through several times, and spent hundreds of hours studying its message and content. I carried my Bible to school and read it at every opportunity. After school I would arrive home as quickly as possible so that I would have more time to drink from its fountain of life, bringing healing and strength. I came to have a certain knowledge that my life and future would be inextricably bound up with the witness of Scripture's message and meaning. There would continue to be a magnetic drawing to preaching being the spoken Word, and to the Bible as the written Word. I had come to share the Apostle Paul's attraction to the proclamation of the Gospel when he affirmed: "For since, in the wisdom of God, the world through wisdom did not know God, it pleased God through the foolishness of the message preached to save those who believe" (1 Co. 1:21). Whereas preaching has often been relegated to the realm of the foolish for much of mankind, it has always been held in the highest regard by God.

Even though the Bible was taking on a greater significance in my life, I was not at all aware of what was germinating in my spirit. For almost the whole year as a fifteen year old boy, I was sensing that God was turning some of that mysterious Word into a new, but frightening self-realization. With ever increasing intensity the power of the Word was laying claim to my life and destiny. I felt God, Himself, was addressing me with a mandate that I too was to be a preacher of that same Word. The Bible was increasingly taking me captive to its claims. On the one hand I recognized that such a call was to be highly cherished, yet I realized that my family heritage made no room for such lofty aspirations or vocational ambitions. There was simply no such history or heritage in my family tree, so what was I to make of such a personal dilemma? I had no historical root system or structural scaffolding for understanding or responding to such a call. Yet, I could not deny that God had laid hold of me for preaching His Word. That inward battle would continue into my sixteenth year. The full acknowledgement of my own personal call to the ministry was just beyond the horizon, but that's another story.

AN EXPOSITIONAL INQUIRY INTO THE TEXT
1 CORINTHIANS 1:19-31

In reference to the text of Scripture by Paul in 1 Corinthians 1:19-31, Paul is setting forth the radical contrast between the words, thoughts, motivations and knowledge of the world with that of the word, thought, motivations and knowledge of the Word of Christ. The phrase "wisdom of this world" (1 Co. 1:20) is Paul's phrase for the ideas, opinions and philosophies of man that has become etched into the thoughts and worldviews of humans and their cultures. These worldly views and beliefs were what the world system, under Satan's rule, embraced and promoted. It was this corrupted wisdom that kept all man's false religions and philosophies energized and promulgated. This worldly wisdom represented and reinforced this message to its cultural constituency throughout the nations of the earth from the beginning of mankind's fall (Gal. 3: 22; Col 2: 8; 2 Th. 2: 7).

The history of man has been directed by human *hubris* (prideful rebellion). Therefore, under the direction of his own arrogance and willfulness, man devised his own concepts, customs and cultures reflecting his sinful choice to live outside the direct rule of His Creator (Gen. 9:1, 10:32, 11:4, 9; Acts 17:24-30). Under the direction of their own darkened minds and the devil's dominion, all the nations devised their strategies for self-rule and structured their societies for self-government apart from God. Each nation or ethnic grouping was conceived, birthed and developed from the so called "wisdom of the wise" (1 Co. 1:19). Therefore, humanity cut itself off from the source of God's revealed knowledge and chose all that was false (Rom. 1:18-32). These beliefs and philosophies became humanity's shared convictions of what was true and real; the tragedy was that the world through its own "wisdom did not know God" (1 Co. 1:21), indeed, could not know God.

For the above reason God chose Abraham for the distinct purpose of breaking this cycle of corrupt nations and for correcting the perversions of all their destructive beliefs and behaviors. God's calling upon Abraham was to raise a redemptive nation and a missionary people to declare His righteousness, goodness and grace to the other nations (Gen. 12:2-3; Rom.10:11-12; 9:30-32). But, alas, even Israel misunderstood her missional and redemptive purposes and perceived her covenant call as recipients of divine blessing while neglecting her covenant call to be a blessing (Gal. 3:6-9). Rather than Israel living the covenant life of faith, she settled for a legalistic existence of bondage to law. She took her God-given heritage as her national birthright to ethnic superiority (Mt. 2:10-12; 3:9-10; 10:5-6; Mk. 11:17). She so lost touch with her calling that, by the time of Jesus, Jewish theology was so confused that the coming Messiah was perceived as being a ruler that would destroy the other nations, rather than being a Savior to all the peoples of the earth. She embraced the privileges of her call while rejecting the responsibilities of that call (Acts 7:51-53; 13:42-47; 17:1-4).

One thing that characterized Paul's background, training and experience was that he was a student of the world's knowledge and an observer of the world's situation (Gal. 1:13-14; Acts 22:3). Paul was a student of cultures and worldviews and therefore could discern and discard what did not fit with the revelation of God in Christ (Gal. 1:11-12; Rom. 10:1-4). When it came to exposing and analyzing the diversity of worldviews, Paul was an expert. He understood that all the cultures surrounding him were to be appreciated, yet approached cautiously and adopted selectively. They all had to conform to and be confirmed by the revelation of God's Word and the Spirit's direct guidance (Acts 17:16-23, 19:8-10).

Before his conversion, Paul realized that in order for him to be a good promoter and evangelist for his Jewish beliefs, he had to understand his multicultural society as well as be an ardent proponent of his own ethnic Jewish faith. Paul was a true representative of his times, for he had a thorough grasp of both the Greco-Roman and Judaic cultures. As a product of these two cultural stories, his heritage represented and reflected both (Gal. 1:14; Acts 13:1; 22:3). The combined learning of these two worldviews produced in Saul of Tarsus the wisdom of the world and drove him to become the fanatical preacher of the rabbinic traditions. The seeds of both Greek wisdom and pharisaic legalism that Saul preached created within him a darkened and violent mind. In addition to this, the historical and depraved womb that produced those cultures shared a common genetic code that left mankind wrongly informed, unsaved and bound for historical and eternal destruction (Rom. 3:9-18; 5:12). However, it was this same unique combination that also allowed Paul to become the great spokesman of the Gospel to all the distinctive cultures, worldviews and religions of his day. He understood that the Gospel of Jesus Christ had to become enculturated into diverse ethnicities without losing its unique and core message (Acts 15:1-5).

Paul's faith encounter with Christ became the catalyst for the rewriting of his own spiritual narrative and destiny. The plotted story that had been scripted for him by the enemy of all souls, took an unintended pause when Paul heard the preaching of a young man named Stephen (Acts 7). As he watched that most unlikely young preacher die that day, Paul began to question the paradigm (radical Pharisaic traditions based on the Jewish Talmud not the Torah) he had lived by and slowly began to allow a new seed to take root and grow. One could also state that a new message got inscribed into his consciousness. Later that new message came into fuller clarity as Christ's Word became encoded into a new, redeemed nature. He began to live out a completely different and new destiny after his Spirit-arranged encounter on the road to Damascus (Acts 9:1-18).

From that time forward, new information of a divine nature began to be inscribed upon the DNA of his human heart. The Word of God preached by Stephen completed its divine cycle by giving birth to yet another new creation in Christ Jesus. The good seed of the Word of God Incarnate produced after its own kind and gave to the world another preacher of the Kingdom. This man named Paul became such a follower of Christ that he wholeheartedly embraced the call to preach the same message of truth and power that had changed him (Acts 9:20-22). Preaching the Word of God became his reason for existence as he sensed that the proclaimed Word (1 Co. 1:17) shared a common genetic link with Jesus who "was the Word, and the Word was with God, and the Word was God" (John 1:1).

Paul realized that, just as there was a connection between the world and the wisdom it propagated, so there was a Spirit-directed commonality between the Word preached and the Word that spoke worlds into existence (Col. 1:16-17). That Word still speaks through the words of the preacher, and it continues to have the same power to change the old into the new. It continues to create a new present through the miracle of new birth, healing in our bodies, deliverance from demonic influences, signs and wonders and miracles of every kind (Rom. 10:11-14; 1 Co. 1:21). Yes, preaching is often categorized as foolishness to the mind of man, but to God and all true followers of Christ, it is still or at least should be "the power of God" (1 Co. 1:18).

The word for "wisdom" in this particular text (1 Co. 1:19-31) is *sophia.* In Paul's day it referred to either the abstract rational principle of the universe (Greek Philosophy), or the cosmic rule of law within the universe (Jewish Torah). The former was an impersonal life force; the latter representing the cause of natural order. The preaching of the Gospel was the personal involvement of God in Christ even unto death on the cross (Phil. 2:5-11). This Gospel was not an impersonal and uncaring energy nor was it just a lifeless principle for ordering the universe; it was and is a personal relationship with the very One who has planned for our ultimate purpose (Eph. 1:4-6).

Therefore, the Gospel of Christ represented a corrective word to all the major cultural philosophies of that era, for Christ was both, God's personal wisdom for mankind and His cosmic passion for the universe (1 Co. 1:24; 2:1). As God's very expression and image of Himself (Phil. 2:6; Heb. 1:3), Christ was the divine principle of God's personal wisdom and thereby greater than all the concepts of human reasoning and was therefore not "foolishness". Also, as the transcendent and eternal Word (John 1:1), God chose to assume human flesh (Eph. 2:15) and therefore should not be considered a "stumbling block" (1 Co. 1:23).

The word for "foolishness" in this passage is *moras.* That God would become man or that heaven would have direct commerce with earth is foolishness only to those whose minds are bound to the logic of fallen reason. Only by the faculty of faith alone can the dichotomy between the supernatural and natural be dissolved; it is only to the natural mind that such a truth is irrational (2 Co. 4:3-4). The revelation that the Kingdom of God has arrived in power through the person of Jesus Christ for both the present and the future, is more than the fallen mind can comprehend (Mt. 10: 7-8; 16:19; 1 Co. 2:14; 2 Co. 3:14). The very idea that Biblical salvation encompasses our whole being of spirit, soul and body is more than the human intellect can absorb. The very thought that we can have a hope that extends to both time and eternity (1 Th. 5:23) goes beyond our finite comprehension. To the worldly wise and legalistic mind, such a message of hope is worthy only of scorn, abuse, rejection and persecution (Acts 4:1-3, 14-18; 12:1-3; 16:16-24). Do not the exact same hurdles exist today as we consider the vain philosophies and false religions in our world and even within our own country? Is doubt and rejection of the whole Gospel not prevalent in the midst of the Institutional Church? Could the idea of inadequate confidence in the power of the Word be alive and well even in us today?

These false attitudes and feelings are reflected in the expressions of all works based religions as seen in the cults as well as in most of the Liberal historic denominations. These reactions are also deceptively camouflaged within the ideas and rhetoric of most secular thinking and animistic religions. Although these last two categories are at opposite ends of the worldview spectrum, they share a common rejection, with regard to, the Gospel's message of hope and grace. Modernism is also frustrated by the Gospel of salvation because it has deified human rationality, while postmodernism has deified human experience. Only the Gospel of the crucified, resurrected and living Lord addresses and corrects the excesses of all these philosophical and religious perspectives. Only the Gospel of Christ provides the appropriate matrix for God's truth that is both rational and experiential (Acts 18:27-28; 19:8-12).

The word for "preaching" in this passage is from the verb *kerysso*. This term for preaching refers to its royal nature. It reminds the preacher of his/her high privilege, awesome responsibility and divine authority that is always intricately woven into the very fabric of preaching. The great absurdity and cognitive barrier for an unbeliever is revealed, in that God has chosen the medium of the preacher, the method of preaching, and the message preached to save the world from itself (Acts 2:40; 3:18-19; 1 Co. 1:18; 2:6). In ancient times royal ambassadors went throughout the land and proclaimed not just the demands of the king, but also the joyous benefits of being under the king's rule. All citizens of the kingdom could expect the blessings of the king as demonstrations of his authority and abundance. The king's emissary was indeed a messenger of Good News (2 Co. 5:20-21; Eph. 6:20).

As ambassadors of Christ our King, we must announce that the Gospel is also Good News for every aspect of our common humanity. He is, indeed, the Savior of our spirit person and the restorer of our mind and emotions and he is even the solution to our rebel will; but He is also the Healer of our bodies and the Mender of every relationship. Those who preach the Gospel are under a divine mandate to anticipate God's supernatural power and glory to be made manifest to the whole person through the event of preaching (Luke 9:1-2; 10:9, 17-20; 24:48-49). It is also our responsibility to teach and encourage the people of God to maintain a high level of expectation from the act of preaching (Luke 1:1-4; Acts 1:1).

I truly believe that there are still only two options left for our deteriorating and misguided world. Either we continue to perish or we to revitalize New Testament preaching and witness. The choice is still to preach or to perish (1 Co. 1:18). To perish means to continue on the collapsing course of the natural world (1 Co. 2:6) and the thinking of the unredeemed mind. Our other option is to encourage the kind of proclamation and witness that begins to move in the rhythm of heaven (Mt. 6:10; 8:16-17;13:11, 23; 14:17-21) and in accord with the drum beat of the Spirit (John 14:12, 26). To preach means to jump into the miraculous flow of the river of life and declare the complete Gospel that liberates people at every level of their lives. At a time when many are most adamant about the dynamic force of the written Word and the legitimacy of the preached Word, the Church needs to affirm the potency and vitality of both (Heb. 2:1-4; 4:12).

At this moment as I sit looking out upon the Shenandoah River, I am thankful for its beauty and force. I can see its dynamic flow and sense its dramatic power, but seated here I have only a limited view and only a restricted knowledge of its reality. My vision of its possibility is somewhat heightened when I observe others canoeing or rowing in the flow of its current, for I can imagine the sights and sounds they enjoy as they float past the river's diverse scenes and feel its surging energy. Their experiences are no doubt greater than mine as I watch from a distance and I can appreciate their increased excitement. But there is one remaining option for me and that comes when I also take the plunge into the river and experience for myself the exuberance and significance of the moment (Ezek. 47:1-9; Ps. 46:4; Rev. 22:1; John 7:38). The pressing challenge today for those who preach or bear witness to the Gospel means that we too plunge into the river of the Spirit's supernatural presence and preach with a renewed expectation of all God's supernatural demonstrations.

Recently I was reading the latest work by the atheist and professor of physics Victor Stenger who delights in expounding upon his contention that God's existence has been thoroughly disproved by Science. He persistently denies all evidences of intelligent design, the divine source of biological complexity, the physical fine-tuning of the universe and the geological anthropic principle. [1] Stenger discounts all natural evidences of God's supernatural involvement in the universe because they do not fit with his atheistic presuppositions. He rejects them because they show, or at the very least they strongly suggest, that the earth's creation and all its natural laws collaborated to make only this planet habitable. Stenger arrogantly asserts "that by this moment in time science has advanced sufficiently to be able to make a definitive statement on the existence or nonexistence of God."[2] Yes, the Gospel of Christ is still being constantly challenged by those who consider the message of the cross absurd and foolish, but the greatest antidote to such poisonous deception is the message of the cross that brings healing to body, soul and spirit (1 Co. 1:18-20).

One can only stand amazed at such prideful idolizing of the scientific method. However, it should be noted that Stenger is only one of many new militant and bold atheists that stake their claim against God and His purposeful creation. I believe that it is a positive and ultimately faith building endeavor to know about atheists like Richard Dawkins, Sam Harris and Christopher Hitchens and to recognize with sadness, their misguided thinking. In this way, we can be aware of the true nature of our mandate and offer them up to God in prayer, binding the forces of darkness that keep them spiritually blind. Thank God for scientists like Hugh Ross and apologists like Ravi Zacharias, who intellectually refute such atheistic arguments (see the last quotes in the next section). However, we need to remain cognizant that the most effective response is for believers to bear witness to our supernatural Gospel with the empowerment of the Spirit.

As I read texts by those who oppose God's creation, the biblical revelation or Christ's redemption, I don't get as agitated with them as I do with us believers who have experienced the truth and power of the Spirit, but don't move in it sufficiently to convince the uninitiated. There are those who reject God because of some childish disappointments, while some go off on emotional outburst for the sake of shock value. Others lash out at God because they are psychologically still hurting over some adolescent trauma and there are still a few who simply like to indulge in their own god-complex. But, I am convinced that most persons who do not believe embrace their skepticism because they have simply not seen the real God evidentially. They have heard us talk enough, but they have not experienced the genuine manifest presence of Christ nor have they had the opportunity to experience the God of the Bible in His glory. The church as a whole has simply not presented the kind of God worthy of their belief and that may well be our failure as much as theirs.

Of course, there will always be those who remain undisturbed and uninfluenced no matter what the proof or evidence, but for the most part when unbelievers encounter the living and powerful presence of God, they do not remain the same. Preaching and bearing witness to the Gospel in the power of the Spirit is the best way for the door to their hearts to be unlocked. Personally, I don't believe that anyone is thoroughly or sufficiently convinced of God's truth by rational argument alone. Rational apologetics reaches mainly the intellect, but the proof of personally experiencing the supernatural presence of Christ and the miraculous wonders of His Spirit addresses the whole person.

Atheist, agnostic, skeptic and cynic alike have a right to hear and see the Gospel demonstrated as objective evidence. Some will continue to renounce the Gospel as "foolishness" and others will resist it as a stone of "stumbling" (1 Co. 1:23), but then what else is new? Some will continue to hold to their naturalistic philosophies and others may hold fast to their pharisaic orthodoxies, but most people are searching for a compassionate and empowering spiritual presence that is both awesome and authentic. Believers can no longer accept or tolerate status quo religion, consensus theology (believing in something simply because it has become the accepted norm) or counterfeit spirituality. Yes, the message of salvation and the challenge of our witness to the world demands a "truth encounter," but not without its corresponding "power encounter." Therefore, our mandate is both crucial and clear: *Speak The Word! Expect The Wonder!*

SUPPORTING QUOTES RELATED TO THE TEXT

"We have tolerated various forms of mediocrity in preaching and exegesis for too long now."[3]

"Paul was a heart preacher. One of the early church fathers said he wished he could have seen three things: Solomon's Temple in its glory; Rome in its prosperity; and Paul preaching."[4]

"Surveys continue to show that churchgoers have high expectations of preaching. When it comes to preaching, hope springs eternal. But the plain fact is that in too many places preaching does not seem to be working well. There is a plague of dullness."[5]

"Paul thus frequently refers to his own effective ministry as a direct result of the work of the Spirit. This work included not only conviction concerning the truth of the gospel, but also signs and wonders, all of which resulted in changed lives."[6]

"In spite of God's obvious blessing and sovereign ordination of many non-Pentecostal ministries, His provision remains for a solid, biblical Christ-centered Pentecostal ministry with signs and wonders. It is not only available, in this present generation it is especially needed."[7]

"By extension in the New Testament age, *Zion* applies to the Church. Just as with Israel, God's purpose for the

Church is that we be the spiritual authority through which Christ can reign and rule; that we proclaim salvation by grace through faith in Christ; that we bind and loose; that we cast out demons; and that the gates of hell do not prevail against us. His desire is for the Church to demonstrate the power and authority of God. Paul and Silas were described as 'men who have upset the world' (Acts 17:6b). Does the world say the same thing about us? Are the power and authority of God on display in the Church today?"[8]

"If 'the cosmos is all that is or ever was or ever will be,' to repeat Carl Sagan's claim, then the fact that it results in the extermination of all life and consciousness also extinguishes the possibility of ultimate hope, purpose, or destiny."[9]

"If the universe really is 'all that is,' as Sagan, naturalist, and secular humanist claim, then what anyone does with his or her life—whether a person lives or dies, loves or hates, gains knowledge or remains ignorant—carries no ultimate significance or purpose whatsoever."[10]

"It turns out that humans arrived right in the middle of the one narrow time window when we can live well *and* see the entirety of cosmic history…One such event may not carry much significance. But when simultaneous 'coincidences' multiply, the 'random accident' interpretation grows less and less plausible and reaches a point at which it must be abandoned."[11]

"Academic degree after degree has not removed the haunting specter of the pointlessness of existence in a random universe. This deep malady of the soul will not be cured by writings such as Harris'. The momentary euphoria that may initially accompany a proclamation of liberation soon fades, and one finds oneself in the vice-like grip of despair in a life without ultimate purpose."[12]

"But even as he rails against God, denying us any transcendent point of reference, he fully embraces God's life-defining prerogatives. His criticisms are caustic, his alternatives bankrupt."[13]

"Routinely, three tests for truth are applied: (1) logical consistency, (2) empirical adequacy, and (3) experiential relevance. When submitted to these tests, the Christian message meets the demand for truth."[14]

QUESTIONS RELATED TO THE TEXT

1. Do you believe there truly is a crisis in preaching today?

2. If you answered "yes" to the above question, what do you see as being the source and focus of that crisis? If you responded with "no", why do you think some have come to that perception?

3. Do you believe there is a difference between the way the early church viewed preaching and the attitude of the church today?

4. According to your observations, what are the corporate perspectives on preaching among the different branches of today's church such as Liberal, Evangelical and Pentecostal?

5. Why do you believe Paul made such a contrasting dichotomy between the wisdom of the world and the foolishness of preaching in his day? To what degree is that dichotomy still true today?

6. When you listen to preachers today do you get the impression that they are more focused on communicating information than on transforming people and their situations?

7. When you preach are you more concerned with "the wisdom of the wise" or with what will be recognized and experienced as "the power of God"?

8. A few years ago William DeArteaga referred to the phrase "consensus orthodoxy". He used the term to refer to "the theological interpretations accepted by most religious people of the day". He explains that Jesus' difficulty with the Pharisees was that they used their consensus orthodoxy to reject any new or fresh work of the Spirit. What are some biblical examples of this kind of flawed thinking? What are some contemporary expressions of this type of false theological reaction to scriptural truth?

CHAPTER TWO

MARK 1:14, 35-39, 2:1-2

~~~~~~

PREACHING WAS HIS PASSION

A NARRATIVE RESPONSE TO THE TEXT

I was sixteen years old and a junior in High School. I was sitting on the living room sofa and in a definite state of bewilderment. I found myself desperately expressing my confusion and anxiety to God. I was verbally crying out to God with both boldness and trepidation. Probably, with more of an inward voice, I let loose with a barrage of frustration: "God is this thing from you or not?" I persisted, "Lord, I've got to know, is that which I'm hearing your voice or another? I continued to insist, "Lord, I need an answer; I need a word from you!" In retrospect, I'm sure my conversation that day with the Lord was not so honoring, but it was honest. It was not the demands of anger, but it was a plea of desperation.

For almost a year I had been privately struggling with that inward sense of a divine compelling, but with little or no thought as to what to do about it. I had absolutely no family history, legacy or environment to help me grapple with such an unsettling and unfamiliar quandary. The unknown quantity presented the question of what or Who was at the source of this mental and emotional anguish? Was this awareness of a divine wooing really from God or was it induced by human desire, selfish motivation or in the now famous words of Scrooge was it simply "a morsel of some undigested bit of meat"? Thus, my need to hear a word of certainty outweighed my moral restraint. The time for polite passivity was over; like Jacob of old, I was prepared to wrestle until my answer came. In Shakespearean terms, my dilemma was to preach or not to preach; truly, that was the question that kept echoing in my mind. I was totally uncomfortable with this frontal approach because of my awe and fear of God and yet I felt that He was just waiting for that kind of spiritual determination and mental desperation on my part.

After presenting my passionate plea for a divine response, I waited. I anxiously thumbed through my Bible and again waited, but nothing happened. I was sure that with such a strong argument or presentation of my case, God could not help but speak a clear word; so I waited but still I received no response. I fully expected God to send an angel on special assignment, to hear His voice thunder in my ear or at the very least to hear that "still small voice" in my mind. Again, I patiently watched for His appearing and waited, but again there was nothing. Having given God, in my own estimation, sufficient time for a reply, I gently tossed my open Bible on the coffee table in front of me. After still another embarrassing pause, I began to suspect yet another period of divine silence. I again waited and just as I feared, no word came. I was losing all hope of any response; my presumed rules of engagement were definitely not working.

Before resolving to dispense with the whole affair, I prepared for a somewhat face-saving retreat from the whole matter. Perhaps my demand for encounter had been ill conceived, naively informed or too hastily selected for obtaining a satisfactory conclusion. Therefore, I decided that my best exit strategy would be to yield my demand to know and simply continue to love and serve God, in spite of my lack of vocational certainty. My next words of surrender were, "Well, Lord, I guess this sense of call is not from you." I continued, "Lord, you surely would not call me to preach. After all, I don't even know how to speak and besides that I'm only a teenager. Who would even listen to me?" The silence was disappointing, and yet there was the comfort of knowing that now I could continue with my own plans. However, I no more than got those self-consoling words out of my mouth, when I casually looked upon my open Bible lying right in front of my eyes.

To my shock and amazement my sight was immediately drawn to the passage opened at the first chapter of the book of Jeremiah. When I chanced a look at the passage before me, my eyes fell directly upon the words of the prophet and his response to God's call. Verse six stood out like a flashing roadside sign, when Jeremiah announced, "Ah, Lord God! Behold, I cannot speak, for I am a youth," (Jeremiah 1:6). I was momentarily greatly surprised, even stunned. Immediately, I realized that Jeremiah's response was essentially the same as my response had been a moment before. Still somewhat shocked by what I considered to be a defining and clear address to me, I knew that God had spoken. As assuredly as God had responded to Jeremiah, I believed He had personally addressed me. I was encouraged, even compelled to pursue my exploration of that passage of Scripture. Intrigued by the similarity of my predicament with that of the prophet of old, I became excitedly drawn to that chapter for further investigation.

I looked up to read the entire context of that particular text to see if there were further commonalities between our life stories. Sure enough, Jeremiah's personal doubts about his own individual worthiness and his doubts about God's direct concern for his situation generated a personal connectedness to my desperate plight. Even in the midst of my suspicions that God would even risk giving a call to someone like me, I began to sense His personal favor. Unlike Jeremiah, I had no such kindred credentials or family pedigree, and yet my eyes became glued upon God's further words to Jeremiah: "Before I formed you in the womb I knew you; Before you were born I sanctified you; I ordained you a prophet to the nations," (Jeremiah 1:5). God's reply to Jeremiah's reluctance was, "Do not say, I am a youth. For you shall go to all to whom I send you. And whatever I command you, you shall speak," (Jeremiah 1:7). I was emotionally stunned, but also relieved for I knew that God, in His own time and in His own way, had spoken a decisive and deliberate word to me.

In retrospect, it seemed that the entire conversation between God and Jeremiah had been His dialogue with me. In a very real sense, Jeremiah's story had become my story. His call became my call. That text became what one could acknowledge as the DNA of my life-long call. I knew in that moment of time that God had spoken through Scripture to affirm His call upon my life. From that day on, I picked up my Bible with the certain knowledge that my destiny was to preach and bear witness to God's Word, in any way and by any means, possible. I was convinced and resolute. There was no longer any doubt or question. My desperation had now turned into a determination to fulfill His call in spite of my youthfulness and unworthiness. Of course, I didn't have a clue what such a call really meant, but ever since receiving the certainty of that initial call, I have never wavered. I knew only one thing for sure; for the rest of my life, my destiny would be inextricably linked to the ministry and proclamation of God's Word.

As I reflect back upon that divine encounter with God, I am still in awe of the phrase where God informed Jeremiah that, not only had He called him but that He had done so even before Jeremiah had been formed in the womb (Jer. 1:5). I continue to be overwhelmed at the thought that God had not only taken notice of my otherwise insignificant conception, but that His call was upon my life before I was even born. The very idea that God had already purposed His plans for me before birth has always given me a life-long sense of divine destiny and responsibility. That sense of God's divine foreknowledge, even of my pre-natal existence, continues to enhance my recognition that all of God's saints are born with God's destined design encoded into their genetic make-up. The Spirit has already done the potential programming within our physical nature by grace; He is simply awaiting our response of faith.

We determine our own destinies through choices, but God in Christ has already designed His preferred outcome for us from the beginning. The word used in the New Testament for this idea is the word *teleioo* which "specifically refers to the object of bringing something to its designed goal."[1] I believe that from the moment we are conceived, God implants His *teleos,* or design, within us so that we can potentially fulfill the goal for which He created us. This word relates to the final cause for which we were created, but the implication is that the desired results have already been imprinted into us by divine design, although the decision to yield to Him is still ours to make. Patrick Glynn writes, "For example, an oak tree (or rather its 'essence' or 'nature') is the final cause of the path of growth that begins with the acorn. The essence of the flower is the final cause of the process that begins with the seed. The essence or nature of the adult human being is the final cause of the process that begins with the fetus in the womb."[2]

This idea of *teleos* is expressed by Isaiah when He acknowledges God as the One "Declaring the end from the beginning and from ancient times things that are not yet done" (Isa. 46:10). In relationship to each person's conception, the psalmist records, "Your eyes saw my substance, being yet unformed. And in your book they all were written, the days fashioned for me, when as yet there were none of them" (Ps. 139:16). How marvelous is God's intentions for us, in that He has already written into our genetic code all that is possible for us to become in Christ. This term *teleos* also relates to the force and power that exist within God's Word to work within us (1 Jn. 2:5; Lk. 12:50). It will be my contention throughout this volume that this great and awesome possibility and power resides within the simple event of bearing witness to the Word of God. Coming to understand this aspect of my own call and the nature of the Word is a constant encouragement to me as I often reflect on that early encounter with the voice of God. Those moments have served as a pinnacle experience in my journey with Christ.

The memory of that previous two-way exchange with the Lord has sustained me in times of discouragement, even as it has forged within me an indelible confidence in Christ's ongoing grace. That divine encounter has also strengthened my own sense of worth in spite of my undeniable inadequacies. Even though that was fifty-five years ago, my focus is still the same, to "preach the Word" (2 Ti. 4:2). Since the time of that call, preaching and teaching God's Word has been my passion. However, it is not just my high esteem of preaching that engulfs me, there is also a holy haunting and human angst in realizing that I have not yet plumbed the depth of the Word's Spirit-empowered potential. According to the Bible, Jesus had the same passion for the event of proclamation, because He like no other operated and modeled just that kind of preaching. His proclamation resulted in continual and consistent miracles and supernatural wonders. He knew the full effect of what the Word of God could achieve and all it was capable of producing. I believe that we who communicate His word must remain dissatisfied until we see His word having the same fullness of effect for which it was intended (Jn. 14:12).

AN EXPOSITIONAL INQUIRY INTO THE TEXT
Mark 1:14, 35-39; 2:1-2

The Gospel of Mark is, I believe, the best book in the Bible to express that preaching and teaching the Good News was also Jesus greatest passion. For the above reason, my favorite Book in the Bible is the Gospel of Mark. I always thought that my choice was based on the author's passionate style, his perpetual motion, his dramatic flair and his consistently dynamic flow from beginning to the end. Now, I realize that those aspects are only the surface reasons for my attraction to this book. The more I read this Gospel account the more I recognize that my preference has more to do with substance than with style. It has more to do with the revelation of Jesus' deliberate purpose than with His rapid pace.

Mark's theme is, in this writer's assessment, "Jesus came to Galilee, preaching the gospel of the kingdom of God."(Mk. 1:14). It was preaching that stood out as the key behind Jesus' sense of urgency.

The best human description of Jesus ministry was that of preaching. Wherever Jesus went, He was there to preach. Whatever else He came to do, His priority was to preach. Jesus was focused upon preaching, for that seems to have been His own self-assumed purpose of existence. Without apology or hesitation He urged, "Let us go into the next towns, that I may preach there also, because for this purpose I have come forth," (Mk. 1: 38). How could Jesus have been clearer regarding His divine and human mandate? Although, He was the Savior of the world, He was a servant of the Word and His message begged to be preached. To Mark the withholding of such truth would be the world's greatest tragedy, for Christ's words represented healing and delivering power, as well as redemption (Mk. 1:39, 42, 45).

For Mark, Jesus was so identified with His servant role that a genealogy could add nothing to His high calling as a preacher and witness of the Word. This Spirit-given view of Jesus' function on earth reveals Jesus' high view, not only of the Eternal Word of God that He personally represented, but also of the preached Word of God that He personally and continually proclaimed. One cannot but be amazed at Jesus' whole-hearted confidence in the written Word, after all it was the Holy Spirit that had inspired and transcribed it. Jesus realized, I believe, that each of the above expressions of God's Word held an individual uniqueness, but they all shared the same Holy Spirit essence and were all expressions revealing a common divine encoding.

Jesus seemed to be of a mindset that if He could just preach God's life-giving revelation, wrongs could be righted, sicknesses could be healed, evil could be halted and the devil's schemes destroyed. He knew that such victory over dark forces would only be partial and temporary, but it would at least point to and emphasize Satan's dethronement at the cross. Jesus' mighty acts were also signs that signaled the devil's total destruction in the *eschaton* or at the end of time. Jesus seemed to be of the mind that announcing His Good News would have both an immediate effect on all of the devil's works and a continuing impact toward completing God's purposes in the earth (Mk. 9:1; 13:10, 31; 14:62). Preaching the Gospel of the Kingdom would result in the manifestation of kingdom realities. Preaching the Kingdom of God would usher in demonstrations of miracles and wonders the likes of which had never been seen (Mk. 2:12; Mt. 11:2-5). Christ's authoritative words and mighty works would be His messianic signs and tokens for the true new age of the Spirit.

Jesus apparently believed that preaching the Kingdom of God carried such spiritual force that it would result in the awesome intrusion of supernatural acts. Jesus' ministry reflected that reality constantly. When He opened His mouth to declare the Word, God's supernatural works followed. Jesus preached and amazing things happened. Jesus preached and demons were cast out. Jesus preached and people were healed of all kinds of sicknesses. Jesus preached and the air became electrified with joy and excitement. Jesus preached and people glorified and worshipped God. Jesus preached and the whole atmosphere became charged with hope and confidence. Jesus preached and lives, attitudes and motivations were gloriously changed and transformed. It is this author's opinion that Jesus allowed nothing to get in the way of His speaking the Word because He knew its ability to change human hearts, human circumstances, human conditions, and human destinies.

Why does Mark open chapter three with Jesus' preaching and teaching ministry in the synagogue? It was well established that the synagogue was one of the key places designated for exhorting, reading and teaching the Word of God. Unfortunately, it had become a place where rabbinic traditions, scribal expertise and commentary interpretations were more highly esteemed than the Word of God itself. God's dynamic words and mighty works were no longer expected, purposed or even desired. God's miraculous presence had long since become simply a subject of discussion, a celebrated memory of another time or a cerebral concept for depriving the present of its possibilities. The synagogue and even the Temple had become places for memorializing the historical past rather than celebrating God's present reality (Mk. 3:2-6; 6:1-2; 11:15-17; Mt. 21:13-14).

The synagogue was a place, not where the God of all revelation and power could be worshipped, but where He could be made a topic of theological debate. It was an area for much talk about God, but where no plans were ever made for His actual arrival or present activities. The ancient God of heaven was acknowledged, but the Living God would not be tolerated and even less desired (Mk 12:27). Neither the synagogue nor the Temple were places where lives were expected to be transformed by the Word nor were they locations where God could make Himself known through awesome signs and wonders. No wonder demons felt at home there. It was a great place for dark spirits and demonic beings to hide out without detection, that is until Jesus came on the scene. It was no wonder that the religious holy places were no longer recognized centers for meeting human needs (Mk. 1:21-27).

As a rabbi, Jesus was a welcome guest wherever He went, although He did not have the scribal education that was considered official training. The people, immediately sensed His genuineness and authenticity (Mk. 1:32-34). Because of His then current popularity, Jesus had been invited to read from the Word and even to teach about God, that is, as long as He spoke only of the God who once did marvelous things. As long as Rabbi Jesus discoursed about the God who was and of His former glory He would be welcomed and even applauded (Luke 4:16-17, 20-22, Mt 23:2; Acts 3:22-23; Deut. 18:15-19; Mk. 12:38-39). When He began, however, to identify Himself and His Father as the living and active God, His popularity began to change. That is the place in His ministry where Jesus' rabbinic similarities ended and His Spirit-led servant's role took over. Rabbi Jesus had no interest in promoting a God who once had all power and who could at one time in the distant past, perform great and mighty acts. This rabbi of the common folk dared to remove God from the dusty trophy case of the historic past and allow Him to breathe and speak afresh in the Market place, on the hill side, in the synagogue and any place He was invited (Mk. 2:1-12).

Jesus arrived on the historical scene however, not to do what had always been done, but to speak and do what His Father was now doing (John 5:17; 8:28). Jesus knew, as the saying goes, 'if you continue to do what you've always done, you'll continue to get what you've always gotten'. It was not accidental that Jesus started His teaching and miraculous ministry by casting out a demon in this particular Gospel. Jesus wanted to disclose the fact that the power of God's Word had dominion over the world of all evil forces. The casting out of demons was often recognized as the epitome of Jesus' Kingdom rule: "But if I cast out demons by the Spirit of God, surely the kingdom of God has come upon you," (Matt. 12:28; Mk. 3:26-27; 14-15). The casting out of demons was often lifted up as the epitome or the signature summation of Christ's ministry on earth. Jesus' personal dealings with demonic beings would be the historical pointers toward the dramatic enactments of Christ's final and climatic defeat of Satan (Acts 10:38; 1 John 3:8; Luke 10:17-18; Rev. 1:17-18; 19: 11-16).

Christ's very words had the ability to cast out and trample on the demons and dark powers. He even gave the same kind of power to His twelve disciples (Mt. 10:1) and a short time later gave it even to the seventy that they might also go out and attack the strongholds of the devil (Lk. 10:19). Why, in Heaven's name, would He not give the same ministry weapon to His disciples today (Heb. 13:8)? Why should God's Word have less intrinsic value, assaulting power and militant force today, since the diabolical enemy is just as determined as he was then (Acts 1:8; Mk. 16:17-18)? Although every age and generation has its own unique satanic tricks and schemes to combat, the case can be made that in these end-times our adversary has stored up some contemporary weapons in his armory. For two thousand years he has been collecting his deadly arsenal for just this unique period of time for even he must recognize that his time is short (Rev. 12:12). But, all Bible believers know that the god of this world (Eph. 2:2; 2 Co. 4:4; John 12:30; 1 John 4:4) will not just lay down his arms easily and retreat into the night. No, that old lion (1 Peter 5:8) must be driven from his lair and held accountable for his murderous ways. Praise God, the weapons of our warfare are still "mighty in God for pulling down strongholds" (2 Co. 10: 4). The Word of God will always have the devastating means of demolishing the devil's works by the mighty works of the Spirit (Mk. 5:1-15; 16:20).

Our text in Mark sets forth an established pattern that Jesus followed in His ministry. He preached and supernatural results followed. Supernatural manifestations took place wherever Jesus appeared and those events, in turn gave Him yet another platform for preaching (Mk. 1:28, 37, 45). Preaching and miracles formed a normative model and recognizable strategy for advancing the Gospel of the Kingdom. In fact, this pattern is also meant to be the anticipated program of the Kingdom through the life and ministry of the Church (Acts 16:27-33). In the words of Michael J. Quicke, "when Jesus Christ came proclaiming (Mark 1:14), his primary concern was not to impart new information but to announce a new way of living in his kingdom."[3] This new way of kingdom living is expressive of the fact that Christ delights in punctuating our natural routines and even our weekly homiletic format with His supernatural interruptions (Mk. 2:2-5; 5:35-36).

The way Jesus functioned and His method of operation is, or should always be, our model. Jesus, Himself, encouraged us in this endeavor when He exhorted the disciples that "he who believes in me, the works that I do he will do also; and greater works than these he will do, because I go to My Father," (John 14: 12). It is fair to say that we often fail to come up to the level of Jesus confidence in us, but our ineffectiveness does not change the normative standard He set for us. Our recognition of failure in measuring up should ignite a greater passion in all who preach and spark within a desire to press on in greater confidence and expectation. God will not honor our pride, arrogance or boasting, but He will honor His Word and our faith expectancy (Acts 3:1-10; 4:12-16; 8:1-4, 5-8).

Even the Apostle Paul admitted: "Not that I have already attained, or am already perfected; but I press on, that I may lay hold of that for which Christ Jesus has also laid hold of me," (Phil. 3: 12). It is exegetically incorrect to assume that Paul is only expressing his future hope in this verse. His future perfection at the resurrection is always a driving force for him, but contextually Paul is speaking more to the existential completion of his ministry call. The point of Paul's life and ministry was that Christ would be magnified either by his life or death. (Phil. 1: 20). Why did Paul take this position as a preacher? Jesus was unmistakably his example and model. If the Gospel is our mirror for detecting our flaws, then it is also our means of eradicating them. The message of the Bible is not just a diagnostic tool for our human predicament; it is also God's medicinal remedy for our sinful condition (Mk. 7:21-23; Rom. 3:19-22). The message of the kingdom is truly God's holistic healing for spirit, soul and body, for that is what preaching is and that is what preaching is meant to do (Mk. 6:2, 31-42; Acts 5:17-20).

In speaking of the healing power of the Word, I am reminded of just such a situation in my own life. I experienced His healing even before I believed that God's healing activity was for today. I distinctly remember that it was the preachers' illumination of Scripture that quickened my own intense search of the Bible. Those formally untrained but anointed preachers that I grew up under, so made the written Word come alive to my young ears that I had to find out more about this mysterious but revered book for myself. For lack of a better phrase, during my teens I became addicted to reading the Bible. I experienced a persistent and unquenchable hunger for the persons, ideas and stories in the Bible. Those early preachers had opened up a whole new world to the previously limited boundaries of my conscious awareness.

All through Elementary School and the first two years of High School, I was a very poor student. Before I started reading the Bible, I seldom read anything, simply because I could barely read. To make matters worse, what I did manage to read I could not understand. This influenced my failure to grasp all my other subjects in school, which in turn effected my own self-image and mental maturity. In reflection, I don't believe the difficulty was my attention span as much as it was simply an obvious inability to comprehend what I read. Yet from the very beginning I did not seem to have that problem in reading and comprehending the Bible. After almost a year of intensely reading the Bible, I began to realize an improvement in both my reading and comprehension levels, even in my classes in High School. Actually, the reality didn't occur to me until after many of my teachers mentioned my vast improvement. My mental grasp of class material, along with a new drive for academic pursuit and a growing apprehension of the Bible, became apparent to all who knew me.

Constant reading of the Scriptures not only gave me a new vision and hope for my life, but was even providing the means of achieving those goals. Out of a family of seven children, only my oldest brother had finished high school, consequently the idea of going to college was never a consideration for any of us. Just finishing high school seemed to be a monumental achievement for members of my family. My background told me that finishing high school was all I had a right to expect or envision, but something was not only happening in my spirit and dreams for the future, something had literally happened in my physical brain. The only way I can describe what was happening was that those brain cells which had been lying dormant for all those years began to revive and rejuvenate. I realize that some might say that I was simply experiencing the normal maturation of adolescence, and that may have been partially true, but I personally choose to give God the praise for the results. The changes were simply too radical and unexpected to be natural sequences. I believe that the Spirit had literally released sparks of healing radiation into my brain cells, that ignited a new passion and determination, to match my new purpose and destiny.

God's mode of operating, I believe, is to work both naturally and supernaturally in every area of our lives. Although I recognize that God was operating by His common grace, I know in myself that His special healing grace was also involved. It was, I believe, those large doses of God's healing Word that I was daily "inhaling" that resulted in a miracle. My undaunted confidence in the Bible can be better appreciated as we remember what the psalmist declared when he wrote: "He sent His Word and healed them," (Ps. 107:20; Col. 3:16; Heb. 4:12; Isaiah 55:11). If one has experienced such inspiration and powerful effects from both the written and preached Word, why would one not be passionate about its powerful potential for all our needs? In every expression of God's Word, there is an infusion taking place that is able to generate and focus its divine energy upon the area of our human need. The Incarnate Word (Jesus) infuses or transmits His energy into the written word (The Bible) and the written word releases its spiritual dynamic into the proclaimed word (faithful preaching and witness). This procedure is, of course, authored and administered by the work and person of the Holy Spirit (2 Peter 1:21; 1 Peter 1:23; Ezekiel 2:2-7).

Chapter two of Mark's Gospel reports that Jesus, "entered Capernaum after some days, and it was heard that He was in the house. Immediately, many gathered together, so that there was no longer room to receive them, not even near the door. And He preached the Word to them. Then they came to Him, bringing a paralytic who was carried by four men." (Mark 2: 1-3). This Gospel account emphasizes that Jesus' powerful preaching prompted an expectant response for the meeting of human needs. This passage also indicates that Jesus allowed His forceful preaching the appropriate time and opportunity to perform and produce its awesome results. It should also be noted that Jesus did not become offended when His preaching was interrupted by those who were determined to get the paralytic an appointment with the Great Physician. It was even as if He was anticipating it.

It is this reality about the Inspired and anointed Word that still works its wonders. The challenge for us preachers in particular and believers in general is to be as passionate and as expectant as was Jesus, whom we are invited and encouraged to emulate. Even when we fail to measure up totally to His standard, we can be comforted with the knowledge that our pattern is that of Jesus and not some lesser ideal. The key to declaring the Word of God is not that our preaching be perfect but that we will set before our vision God's perfect example and standard.

As ministerial leaders, we must not be content with expecting less from ourselves than the saints may come to expect from us, as bearers of the very Word of God. All that is required of the preacher is so humanly impossible that if God doesn't intervene, no human ability can suffice. Bringing about human change and transformation is so radically impossible that without God's intervention our frail human efforts are worthless. However, let us have the same passion to preach that Jesus had and demonstrated, then be willing to leave the rest up to Him. Our challenge as a believer is to proclaim God's powerful Word and be confident that His mighty signs will follow (Mk. 16:20). By Christ's grace and the Spirit's anointing, *Speak the Word, Expect the Wonder!*

SUPPORTING QUOTES RELATED TO THE TEXT

"Is preaching really worth all the effort? Few in the congregation appear to notice the preacher's diminished commitment--in fact, sadly, listeners almost seem to expect less and less. Spiritual discipline drops a notch or two, and preachers settle for second or third best."[4]

"When we speak of the communication of the gospel, we have in mind the miracle of God's self-revelation in Jesus Christ. Communication rests not on techniques or human strategies but on the divine initiative."[5]

"The gospel is a word that goes out from God and does not return to him empty (Is. 55:11). It is a word that remains the property of God, but a word that we can hear and know through the action of the Spirit of God upon us."[6]

"The renewal of the church will rise or fall on the quality of its preaching, and I think it will depend on preachers who make preaching the central priority in their allocation of time and energy."[7]

"It doesn't matter what I have in my notes to say. It doesn't matter whether I get my favorite point in or not. It matters that I am guided by the Holy Spirit to that precise area of need in the lives of my congregation."[8]

"I am afraid that the church is becoming worldly in its need to come up with something new and different. Anytime something is new we either have to improve it or it deteriorates from what it was before. How can the gospel be improved? How dare we deteriorate what is already perfect."[9]

"They beat Paul half to death—they thought he was dead, and he got up and went to preaching again. Anybody who ever did anything mighty for God had to be relentless."[10]

"Throughout Kathryn Kuhlman's services she encouraged people to believe God for healing. They didn't have to wait for the evangelist to pray for them."[11]

"Until we see that the Father's highest purpose is to reveal in us the nature of Christ, we will not qualify for the power of Christ, which is God's full endorsement upon our lives."[12]

"The danger is to become a professional (in the pejorative sense of the word): to analyze texts and talk about God, but slowly to let the fire of passion for God run low, so that one does not spend much time talking with God."[13]

"The exegetical process is not completed until we return to the proper posture of objects being addressed by the subject."[14]

"We have a generation that is less interested in cerebral arguments, linear thinking, theological systems, and more interested in encountering the supernatural."[15]

"No Christian or church has the right to deviate from the Bible, but each has the freedom to respond to the creativity of the Spirit."[16]

QUESTIONS RELATED TO THE TEXT

1. Is it an unfair expectation to think that the preacher should or can give his highest priority to preaching in a day when there are so many other demands upon the minister?

2. Is it appropriate to press the point in regard to Jesus making preaching His primary purpose, when viewed from the perspective of the entire New Testament?

3. Should preaching and miracles be so closely linked? Why or why not? In what situations might there be an over-emphasis on external miracles?

4. If persons in the pew are expecting less from preaching, what difference can accompanying miracles make?

5. If effective communication of the Gospel depends mainly upon the work of the Spirit, why should a preacher offer his/her human best?

6. How do we, as contemporary ministers, balance the use of modern tools and new technologies with the innate adequacies of the Gospel?

7. The term *kerysso* is considered to be the primary New Testament word for preaching as it relates to the royal dimension of proclamation. It emphasizes both the authority of the one proclaiming the message as a kingly representative and the kingly authority of the one who originally authorized the sending of the message. However, what about words like *euangelizo* or m*artyreo?* See David J. Hesselgrave's text *Communicating Christ Cross-Culturally*, page 25.[17]

CHAPTER THREE

JOHN 3:14-15; NUMBERS 21:5-7; I CORINTHIANS 2:4

SPEAKING THE WORD;
UNLEASHING THE POWER

A NARRATIVE RESPONSE TO THE TEXT

Standing behind the auditorium curtain I was waiting and struggling with a nervousness I had never felt. Finally the teacher in charge of the annual High School talent show came behind the stage curtain and announced to me that I was up next on the performing platform. Many thoughts began to flood my mind, but the one I remember best was "What in the world am I doing up here? What did I get myself into?" It had all previously seemed quite surreal, but now the moment had arrived for an immediate response, for as the phrase goes, "I would have to put my money where my mouth was". I can think of many cliches that fit the moment, but that particular one is sufficient to communicate my dilemma. In a very short time I would be expected to stand before the entire student body of 500 youth, plus 25 teachers. The inward butterflies were really stirred up and quickly multiplying.

It had been my decision to ask for a seven minute slot in the program to preach. I was the one who had boldly pressed the issue to speak to the student body and the directors of the talent show had reluctantly agreed. There I was standing behind those thick blue drapes getting ready to go out on that stage and perform an unprecedented and public act of preaching. That's right, you read me correctly. As far as I knew, no one in the historical annals of my High School had ever made such a request for permission to preach during the annual talent show. Even in the fifties there was a sense of sacredness in the separation of church and state. There was nothing stated, but it was generally assumed that the talent show was hallowed secular ground. Actually I must admit it even seemed inappropriate to me that I should make such a request. However, the die had been cast; my time to intrude into their scheduled "show time" had arrived.

The courage that had existed when I first made the request was rapidly disappearing and I was beginning to feel an emotional melt-down coming on. There was no way I could gracefully back out now and there was no place to run. This defining but terrifying moment was upon me. What was I to do? The reality of being called to preach suddenly took on a stark and frightening new reality. I knew that God had opened this door, but now the issue was did I have the "guts" to go through that door? My heart began to pound and my knees to quiver. Self-doubt and trepidation were on the rise; all confidence was quickly vanishing. Even a teenager with a sense of divine call can be a menacing threat to the powers of tradition and political correctness. In spite of the ominous emotional obstacles in front of me I knew I had to "rush in where angels fear to tread".

This story had begun three weeks earlier. As I was walking out of the main building of the school, I glanced up to see a flyer on the bulletin board, advertising the annual school talent show. Ordinarily I would not have given that announcement a second thought; I had discovered no gifts worthy of public display. I, especially, had no abilities or talents that were polished enough for performance in front of the entire student body. For some reason, that flyer continued to draw me into its message. I couldn't walk away from its alluring and beckoning challenge. Slowly the invitational words on this poster began to take on the need for an evocative and personal response. I began to sense the Lord telling me that I ought to be in that talent show. It would be an opportunity to share the Gospel with the whole school at the same time. They would be a captive audience.

At first I dismissed the idea as being humanly impossible since I thought the school administration would never allow it. Secondly, I reasoned that to be in a talent show, one needed to be talented. Thirdly, I assumed the challenge to be personally infeasible; no teenagers would be willing to endure such a blatant interruption into their routine world, even by one of their own. Fourthly, to even consider such action on my part was just plain scary. However, the thought that I should, at least request the opportunity to preach in that talent show, persisted without let up. The whole idea seemed ridiculous and more than a bit presumptuous, but I knew I had to try.

The inner voice that persisted was not voicing a divine demand or a forced requirement of obedience. The sense of compulsion was that such a kingdom opportunity should not be neglected. I saw the prospect as a spiritual privilege and perhaps as the only opportunity I would ever have to bear witness to my fellow classmates and teachers all at one time and all in one place. Even as a youth I felt a sense of responsibility akin to Ezekiel's watchman on the wall (Ezek. 33:6-9). Someone of their own age needed to make them more conscious of their spiritual need, and right or wrong I felt as if it was my destiny to be the one to stand on that wall and declare the Word. In all truth, that thought didn't make it any easier or any less foreboding.

Within a few days I made my request to the talent show directors to be in the production, and since it was open to all students they could hardly refuse me. It must be noted that their reluctance and lack of enthusiasm was apparent. Their hesitancy was obvious, and I understood and appreciated their dilemma. When asked to list what I would be performing, without hesitation, I proudly and somewhat presumptuously wrote down preaching. The directors of the program were then faced with an obvious difficulty. Everybody knew, including me, that this was not the usual place or time for this kind of activity. My request could have created a challenging situation for the school administration, and yet, to their credit they would not decline my request. Tolerance and school policy would not permit their declining anyone from the talent show. I was reminded, however, that I had to stay within the allotted time limit of seven minutes.

Upon being approved, I knew immediately what Scripture I was to share with my fellow schoolmates. I had such a knowing in my mind that I was certain that the Lord Himself had given me the appropriate passage and felt confirmed that my course had been determined by Heaven itself. My task was to talk about Jesus' conversation with Nicodemus in general, but the specific text was, "And as Moses lifted up the serpent in the wilderness, even so must the Son of Man be lifted up, that whoever believes in Him should not perish but have eternal life," (John 3:14-15). I knew that, like Moses of old, I was to lift up the banner of Christ to my high school audience. I had already become familiar enough with the whole Bible to know that my chosen text had a historical basis found in the story of the children of Israel in Numbers 21:5-9. For the few remaining weeks before the designated day of the talent show, I fervently prayed for strength, faithfully considered the challenge and mentally lived with those passages of Scripture.

I was, of course, apprehensive, but I was undaunted by the sense that mine was a divine assignment. I had no idea how my peers would react to such a brazen act of intrusion into their program of entertainment. I did not wish to invite their mockery, disdain or shunning but I knew I could not neglect this God given mandate.

Finally, the appointed day arrived. I was excited for the opportunity but also glad that the day of my greatest challenge would soon pass. I assumed that I was ready for the task for I knew I was under divine appointment. I was God's own sent messenger and ambassador to present Christ to my classmates in an unprecedented format. But as I stood there, I was unprepared for the stage freight that began to take hold and grip my heart. I assumed I would be apprehensive, but I failed to anticipate the sense of actual fear and dread that would come rushing in when the moment actually came. The unanticipated level of fear would have been paralyzing except for the knowledge that the Word of God could be heard afresh by the entire student body.

The moment of truth had arrived. I was standing on the edge of my greatest challenge and opportunity. In the midst of my nervousness, I knew a moment's relief when one of the adult directors came back stage and told me that they were going to cut me out of the program since the designated time for the event was running too close. It is hard to express the sense of exuberant joy and relief that I felt in that moment. Of course, I had to act disappointed, but inside I was exhilarated and not a little relieved. I consoled myself with the fact that at least I had tried and that I had done my part.

However, I was quick to recognize that now I had an even bigger internal problem. How was I now to deal with the ambiguity? I was so sure I had been hearing from God. How was I to emotionally reconcile the incongruence between divine compulsion and human circumstance? Again, I took refuge in the thought that I had done my best, but even that felt like retreat and compromise. Beyond the temporary relief I felt that the sense of obligation was gone, I now sensed regret that a wonderful opportunity to witness for Christ had been lost.

How quickly this dilemma took me to the brink of doubt trying to figure out how much I could ever trust hearing from God again. I was inwardly stymied and not a little bewildered. Now, my desperation was of a different kind. Had God been speaking or was this all a confusing figment of my own imagination? My response was immediate and deliberate. I quickly found a deserted spot behind one of those big inner velvet curtains and quietly presented my predicament to God. I knew that this situation had not caught Him unaware, so I realized that my anxious little monologue was for my benefit and not because of His surprise.

My paraphrased and prayerful thoughts went something like this: "Now God, you know this was not my idea. I've done only what I thought you were saying, so you will have to work this situation out. I'm willing to do whatever you want, but its now up to You." At that point I felt better and for the moment the decision was in God's hands or as the saying goes the ball was "back in His court". I had no idea what was going to transpire next so I turned around and walked back out to the waiting area with the other performers. Immediately, the same director who had just told me that I was being dropped, came back behind the outer curtain and indicated to me that I was still on the program. In fact, she announced, "You are the next one to go out".

I didn't even have time for further worry. I'm sure I was somewhat in a state of shock, although in the midst of all the program confusion, something had unconsciously changed within me. When the curtains opened up and I started walking toward the lectern, there was no fear or anxiety. The grip of paralyzing bewilderment was broken. Somehow all the nervousness was replaced with a bold confidence and an excitement for what God was about to do through me. For seven minutes I delivered the message that had been burning in my heart for those past weeks. I spoke with forthrightness, deliberateness, simplicity and with a clarity and confidence that surprised everyone, most especially me. I spoke also with genuineness and humility overjoyed with the reality that I was but the clay pot that the Lord had decided to use for His purposes.

It was a strange phenomenon, indeed, for I knew an audience was there, but I was totally focused on the task at hand. The only recognition I had of the sea of faces before me was that they were not distracted or disinterested at all, but rather seemed totally drawn into what was being said. They did not jostle, stir, wiggle or move about, in or from their seats. It was as if they were immersed in a holy atmosphere that could only have been created by the presence of God's Spirit. No one joked, snickered, sneered or smiled condescendingly as I had anticipated. Both the students and teachers seemed to be captivated and drawn into a holy silence and thoughtful hush. It was as if that auditorium had been changed into a freeze frame of suspended animation and super charged with a current of spiritual energy and awe. The Word of God was having its mesmerizing effect even though it was being presented by one of Christ's most unpolished and least gifted servants.

It was a serene and surreal moment that I will never forget, for I knew that it had nothing to do with me. The presence of God's anointing had invaded that public hall and for a few moments had turned it into His hallowed sanctuary. It was as if that ordinary environment had been transported into an extraordinary realm and I was keenly aware that none of it was my doing. The impact of that seven minute sermon delivered by such an inexperienced, untrained and even shy teenager could only have been accomplished through the initiative and visitation of the Spirit. It would be years later before I came to realize that I was not the only one who would remember that day.

When my wife and I went back for my tenth high school reunion, I had several ask me if I remembered that event. I must admit that I was somewhat embarrassed at my youthful tenacity and adolescent forwardness. As an adult, I had often thought back on those moments with shock thinking I had given in to such adolescent inappropriateness. It was also surprising to me that few seemed to remember the winning football touchdowns or the winning baskets of the basketball games, but several remembered the afternoon where one of their own had the audacity to preach the Gospel to them during a high school talent show.

It remains the simple fact that the straightforward declaring of God's Word had unleashed the very power of Christ's presence into that auditorium.

It is most unfortunate that in our materialist and skeptical culture preaching is no longer honored as it should be. In fact, more often than not, it is disdained and considered an outmoded form of communication. Engulfed and entranced by our technological wizardry today, preaching is presumed to be innocuous, ineffective and unworthy of continued use. The passing of time has only increased my confidence in the innate, compelling nature of the Spirit's anointed proclamation of God's Word. I also believe that the more we are willing to step out of our human comfort zone, the more the Spirit will anoint our feeble efforts (Mt 10:19-20). What will be the eternal fruit or consequences of that short seven minute message's impact on my peers? Only eternity will reveal its everlasting results, but in relationship to my own faith and ministry, the memory of that preaching event left an indelible recognition of preaching's potential and the Word's powerful force.

Perhaps there were many who sat listening to the sound of my voice that day and nothing registered on the radar screen of their minds and hearts. It could be that no souls were rescued from the flames of the abyss or it may be that no one made a life-changing decision to follow Christ after hearing that message. The one thing I know is that I was obedient to share a life-giving Word from the Lord and that not one person of those five hundred students could deny that they had heard the Gospel message. A second reality of which I am confident was that the atmosphere of that auditorium had been momentarily touched by the Presence of the Lord. It may well be that the one whose attitude and future that was most impacted was me, because from that moment fifty-five years ago I have maintained an indomitable expectancy in regards to the Holy Spirit's use of God's Word. I am convinced that when we bear witness to the Word, the Spirit releases His energy. When the Spirit and the Word come together there is a dynamic fusion that takes place in the atmosphere around us. The amazing reality is that we, as believers, get to have the honor and privilege of being the contact point for that explosive energy and power by His grace.

AN EXPOSITIONAL INQUIRY INTO THE TEXT
JOHN 3:14-15; NUMBERS 21:5-7; 1 CORINTHIANS 2:4

In looking at the biblical passage in John 3:14-15, I find myself amazed and surprised by the diversity of theological categories within these two verses. First, there is John's drawing of an integral connection with the historical drama, drawn from Numbers 21:5-9, where John records that "Moses lifted up the serpent in the wilderness". Second, in the Gospel passage we are shown the salvational distinctive where John points to the cross as the center piece of the redemptive story, when He relates that "even so must the Son of Man be lifted up". Third, there is the unspoken but very real challenge that this message of the cross must be preached, and must be believed.

Paul unapologetically declares that preaching is integral to the very nature of the cross and the fact of the cross demands the response of preaching (1Corinthians 1:18). It would appear that John is using a play on the words "lifted up," referencing both to Jesus being lifted up on the cross at His crucifixion and to the act of preaching the message of that death by crucifixion. The dynamic of being "lifted up" is John's way of alluding to both the historical means of salvation in the cross and the essential heralding of the message of the cross. The two are forever and inexorably linked together.

Fourth, we note one of John's primary themes of his Gospel when he announces "That whoever believes in Him (Jesus) should not perish but have eternal life" (John 3:15). To this message of Jesus' life and sacrifice there are only two choices. Either, one must believe or doubt, accept or reject, embrace or refuse the Word incarnate and the word preached. This call for response is also Christ's demand for nothing less than an experiential decision. However, the acceptance of Christ is not a mere intellectual decision, a choice of the will, or an emotional response, rather, it is a total surrender that bears within it the promise of a radical renewing of the entire human person beginning with the "rebirth" of the spirit (John 3:3). It is significant to note that this response is a mental function of the human will, but what is most radically apparent is the actual restoring of the human spirit back to its pre-fallen state (Rom. 8:15-16).

This event is not just a philosophical process or a psychological adjustment, it is a revolutionary restoring experience of man's nature, at his or her deepest core and, according to the above passage this experience is testable. In other words, in the realm of the Spirit, the new birth is an empirical reality (John 4:28-29, 39-42). There will be objective and verifiable evidence of the Holy Spirit's work within us; this could be thought of as a Spirit to spirit (John 3:6) interaction that takes place within our human nature.

Finally, this faith act produces such a dramatic crisis and transforming change process that it affects every dimension of a person's present and future. The term "eternal life" was John's designation of the new quality of life that one has in Christ now, as well as the hope of an everlasting life with Christ in the hereafter. Eternal life points to the endless quantity of years that the believer will spend with Christ in Heaven, but also acknowledges the quality of life that the believer now has in Christ. John's term "eternal life" is similar to the Synoptic Gospel's use of the term for the "kingdom of Heaven" or "kingdom of God." All of these scriptural phrases point to a state, condition, sphere or dimension that has both arrived and is yet coming in fullness and brings together both the present and future aspects of biblical eschatology.

In approaching the passage in Numbers 21:5-9, I realized that this Old Testament text is best interpreted in the light of the New Testament. Only by understanding the Gospel text can we better grasp the meaning of the Numbers passage. However, as we allow the latter to inform the former, we can observe some important insights. Verse five says that "the people spoke against God", then further down it says "our soul" detested the bread that God had given from heaven. First, we observe Israel's situation revealed as a collective attitude, but their reactions also represented the results of individual choice. The sin of the people reflected the contagious nature of sin itself, which both corrupts the human nature and keeps it bound to the weaknesses of cultural traditions and fallen ethnic influences.

Second, we see that there was also an external result of their complaining, namely the "fiery serpents" (21:6). These venomous snakes pointed to divine judgment but also represented the very presence of evil itself (Genesis 3:1-15; 1 Co. 10:9). Third, we can determine that the divine solution for Israel in the wilderness is God's permanent answer to the human condition, through Jesus being lifted up (Num. 21:8-9; John 3:14-15). The Numbers passage was a unique picture that encapsulating mankind's hope of salvation. We should never be surpriced by the concept of salvation in the Old Testament, especially as a picture or type which always points to the New Testament reality in Christ (Col. 2:17; Heb. 10:1). Here salvation goes beyond the normal redemptive analogies that we find in the Old Testament; in this passage, it is a serpent on a pole, not a lamb on the brazen altar, blood on the horns of the golden altar, or a slave in the market place that points to redemption. A serpent on a pole is a little more surprising and suggests an expanded dimension to Christ's complete redemption and triumph.

In the Numbers text, the very image of the curse becomes the image of the cure, which is exactly what the scandal of the cross reflected. This reality seems to go beyond the other types in that it points not just to the fact of redemption, but how that redemption was enacted. It suggests Paul's revelation that Christ not only conquered sin, but that He was able to do so because He became "sin for us" (2 Co. 5:21). Therefore, in Christ we are able to receive pardon and power over sin as we also enjoy a new position with Christ (Eph. 2:6).

The salvation emphasis here follows what has been called the *Christus Victor* theme. The very cause of our sickness unto death purposefully became a participant in our victorious deliverance (Rom. 5:17, 20-21). Moses was told to nail a bronze serpent to a pole and hold it up for all to look upon (Zech. 12:10; Ps. 22:13-18; Rev. 1:7). God may have had Moses use bronze to serve as a mirror to reflect back to the people the hideousness of their sin, for bronze was often used for mirrors (Ex. 38:8). The crucified Christ victorious over the serpent, is first presented in Genesis 3:15 where God tells the embodiment of evil, "And I will put enmity between you and the woman, and between your seed and her seed; He shall bruise your head, and you shall bruise His heel."

That same *Christus Victor* legacy is passed on down to every generation of believers as acknowledged in Jesus' words: " Behold, I give you the authority to trample on serpents and scorpions and over all the power of the enemy, and nothing shall by any means hurt you" (Luke 10:19). Also we see the same truth for all believers recorded in Mark 16:18, which describes our power over all the host and works of the devil. In fact, every expression of demonic deliverance in Jesus' ministry is an illustration of His triumph over all forms of evil (Luke 11:20).

The Old Testament text corresponds to the New Testament text in that both adhere to a holistic view of salvation which touches mankind's triune nature of spirit, soul and body. When the children of Israel are told to look upon the serpent on the pole, it is an invitation to life (Num. 21:8). This act of gazing upon the serpent on the pole was at the same time a spiritual deliverance, an emotional victory and a physical cure. It was their obedient response to the voice of God and the Word of life that produced the accompanying wonders of life and healing, to all who would look; their gaze was an expression of their belief (Mk. 15:39). Actually, Paul tells us that it was the pre-incarnated Christ that actually was present in that Old Testament historical narrative (1 Corinthians 10: 9).

In reflection, the profound effect of my high school preaching many years ago, had everything to do with the innate energy of the

Word of God declared.

Also, that Word was reinforced by the fact that the message of Jesus was being verbally lifted up and that the reality of Him was embodied within their hearing. Those young people were literally drawn into the presence of the Lord, because Jesus was lifted up in their midst by the preached Word. In that high school auditorium the Word became event within their hearing and by the power of the Spirit's manifest presence and they were able to experience a measure of Christ's glory (Ex. 25:22; 40:34-35). In the Bible, the Word is never just ideas to be heard, but actual events to be experienced.

In other words, His Message became the means or medium for apprehending the Lord's presence in the midst of an ordinary event. The text of Scripture became a divine manifestation within their normal context by the anointing of the Holy Spirit. The apostle Paul certainly understood this conceptual and experiential component of the Word of God when it had been fused with the Spirit of God. Paul, himself, affirmed, "My message and my preaching were not with wise and persuasive words, but with a demonstration of the Spirit's power" (1 Co. 2:4). The historical narrative became an existential reality in that Spirit-anointed atmosphere.

My preaching was certainly not apologetically persuasive, nor hermeneutically sound, but without my realizing it the preaching moment of the Word became a contextual event of the Spirit. It is my belief that a supernatural encounter with God is meant to be and flow from the natural result and outcome of preaching. The sermon is not so much an exercise for assimilating information or even Christian formation, but is meant to be an experience for encountering the divine presence and power. In fact, spiritual formation, as important as that is, is not so much the result of protracted acquisition of knowledge or educational material, but more the consistent experiencing of God's supernatural manifestations that occur within our natural circumstances.

It is true that preaching should always have a rational component and therefore involve an intellectual apologetic in that, by way of communication it gives an adequate reason and defense for faith. However, from this writer's perspective, Christian proclamation is innately supernatural and is therefore at its best apologetically when it communicates through supernatural wonders. True preaching thrives mainly in the realm of the supernatural, because that is primarily its anticipatory nature. In other words, the preacher's main obligation is to speak and act under the anointing of the Spirit and allow for the continuing work of Christ to flow through that Word (Acts 1:1). Donald G. Bloesch is theologically correct when he warns: "We must avoid both an apologetic accommodationism and a kerygmatic reductionism if we are to give a convincing and biblically faithful statement on the communication of the gospel to the unbelieving world of our time."[1]

Bloesch's statement is appropriate to this writer's perspective on preaching. I understand Bloesch to be saying that bearing witness to the Gospel can not be just reasonable defense or cognitive content. All forms of Christian proclamation should be both a reasoned presentation and a rational defense of the Gospel, however, true biblical proclamation of the Gospel must be primarily *pneumatic* or Spirit-directed and Spirit-energized. Only then will preaching be truly apologetic or kerygmatic. By this I mean that preaching the Word in and by the anointing of the Spirit carries within itself the spiritual energy to convert and to convince because it contains its own validity and vitality.

As Word and Spirit, proclamation becomes the lion let loose to defeat all of its enemies. The Word does its own work when enlivened and directed by the Spirit's power and when Word and Spirit become genuinely integrated we should preach with expectation of miraculous signs and wonders along with a rational and convincing impact. True preaching will be reasonable and cerebral, but its real force lies in what it is able to accomplish beyond the natural realm and cognitive level. God does not want

His Word to rely on or be limited by either mankind's natural gifting or his/her hermeneutical expertise (1 Co. 2:5; 1 Th. 1:5).

SUPPORTING QUOTES RELATED TO THE TEXT

"The gospel needs to be heralded more than defended. It needs to be announced and explicated but not recommended as if it were an item for sale."[2]

"Communication of the gospel involves not simply the imparting of information but the transmission of meaning and power."[3]

"The principle channel of God's redeeming action is the heralding of the gospel...And in the words of 1 Peter: 'you have been born anew, not of perishable seed but of imperishable, through the living abiding word of God... That word is the good news which was preached to you (1 Pet. 1:23, 25).'"[4]

"When it comes to the ministry of apologetics in the local church, the pastor and other leaders must know the way and show the way. They must lead the church by conviction and example in helping people answer tough questions about life...The pastor who ignores the role of apologetics in dealing with these questions will find himself offering compassion without conviction, and comfort without the ultimate comfort of knowing God."[5]

"In the same way, while no single argument will convince an unbeliever of God's existence, the weight of evidence will lead the unbeliever to conclude that God does exist."[6]

"Evangelism today is about existential persuasion as well as intellectual persuasion."[7]

"It's as though the truth of the gospel must be existentially perceived---at least initially---rather than rationally grasped...No amount of well-argued reasons for faith can bridge the existential gap that is created by a lifeless, despondent church."[8]

"I do indeed love apologetics. We should have reasonable ways to defend the authority and authenticity of the Scriptures. But I had become a Christian, not because I finally met someone who could answer all my questions, but because my heart was open and hungry for God. The passion of my heart became a cry to see the demonstration of the power and gifts of the Holy Spirit."[9]

"Power resides in the Word."[10]

"In true Pentecostal preaching, the congregation and the minister act together."[11]

"The nature of Jesus' ministry was threefold: (1) preaching and teaching; (2) exorcism (the casting out of devils) and healing; (3) the training of disciples."[12]

"Preachers are ambassadors of God...They speak with the power and authority of the governments they represent... Back of us, we have the power and authority of heaven. We are, through Him, more than a match for Satan and the powers of evil."[13]

"We live in a visual age. Men and women have short attention spans. They are geared to thirty-second commercials and fast-moving T.V. scripts."[14]

"The first Pentecostal sermon produced miraculous and unprecedented results...Pentecostal preaching today... when following the same pattern, when emphasizing the same points, when directed of the same Spirit, will produce similar results."[15]

"I believe…that Satan attacks us primarily in the area of self-image. He is desperately afraid we will discover who we are and make life difficult for him."[16]

QUESTIONS RELATED TO THE TEXT

1. To what degree does human personality play a part in the preaching of God's Eternal Word?

2. What can the preacher do, if anything, to determine or insure a desired response? What can a preacher do to encourage or influence a supernatural manifestation?

3. One of my favorite definitions of faith is "the willingness to attempt such impossible tasks that if God doesn't show up the project will miserably fail". Is that definition too theatrical or even presumptuous?

4. What is the probability that such a high expectation of the Word of God to perform supernatural intervention might also encourage ministry slothfulness?

5. Is the theme of *Christus Victor* in the expositional inquiry section of this text overstated or even misplaced?

6. Has this chapter overemphasized the kerygmatic or heralding focus of the preaching event? Has the intellectual or rational dimension of preaching been overly diminished in your estimation?

7. To what degree should the local church be concerned about nurturing its members to give rational and relevant answers to the great questions of faith?

8. How much focus should the Church give to rational apologetics? How much should we also be concerned to give an apologetic of the Spirit's supernatural demonstrations?

9. How might our success in witness be greatly enhanced if every believer were equipped with both rational explanation and supernatural demonstrations?

CHAPTER FOUR

GAL. 5:16-17; ROM. 8:16-17; JOHN 3:16

SPIRIT AND FLESH: THE BATTLE IS ON!

A NARRATIVE RESPONSE TO THE TEXT

I couldn't believe that I was so emotionally upset by the news of the death of Kenneth, a member from my former church. Why was I so affected by such a common occurrence in pastoral ministry? My wife and I were newly appointed to a church in the District with exciting professional possibilities. I was only thirty years old but I had been accepted as associate pastor of an eighteen hundred member church with one of the most respected and popular pastors in the central Illinois area. It had even been hinted that I was one of those young ministers being groomed for bigger and better things. I was now a pastor in a great church and positioned for further vocational possibilities along with great potential for ecclesiastical ladder climbing.

Linda and I were expecting our second child and both had good incomes. The town we had just moved to was just perfect. After living in older parsonages for most of our time in ministry, at this new church we were provided with a newer home. I was well received in the community and the church was filled with well-to-do and educated professionals. Added to this, I had just recently achieved the honored rank of black belt in competitive Judo and was invited to start my own Judo club at the local community college; everything was really going great. I guess you could say I felt like Goldilocks in that every thing seemed "just right." I was at the place where many of my goals had been fulfilled even beyond my own expectations. Life was good and appearing to look even better in every measurable way. I was blessed to find that I was experiencing expanded opportunities to grow in every area of ministry. The problem was not with succeeding, but that my focus was being directed more and more toward a worldly preoccupation, materialistic thinking, professional success and the plain pleasing of the flesh. One might say that, without my realizing it, the battle between the flesh and the Spirit was being waged and the flesh was winning.

Since all was going so well, why was I so overwhelmed by the death of a church member from a former church? Death was a reality that I had confronted many times in eleven years of pastoral ministry. Why was I feeling so sad over hearing about this particular church member dying? I knew him well and had spent many hours with him, but it had been several months since I had even seen him. I had been able to minister to him for several months previously and we had built a good friendship; I knew he felt I was a good pastor and one of the good guys, why then was my emotional equilibrium so off balance; the death of church members was not anything foreign to me. His death hadn't even been unexpected. Yet, here I was sitting behind my office desk on a Saturday morning overcome with a sense of the futility and uncertainty of life. Within a few days I was able to push the whole experience of dread back to the periphery of mental awareness. In unguarded moments however, memories of my painful response to a friend's death continued to bubble up into my conscious awareness.

Since I felt my own salvation and my hope of eternity was secure, the overpowering concern about my friend's death was not a matter of contemplating my own demise. I had neither inordinate fear of death nor undue doubts concerning my own heavenly expectations, so why was I so emotionally distraught? In time I began to realize the source of my bewilderment. My anxiety over my friend's death stemmed from the knowledge that, in spite of all the times of personal ministry to him, I couldn't remember any time when I had questioned him about his own personal salvation or readiness to meet the Lord. It wasn't that I didn't consider the question of Kenneth's eternal salvation significant it was simply that I had come to doubt the necessity of asking the question. I had fallen so far into a good works mentality that the biblical idea of being born again had ceased to be an important issue. It wasn't that I didn't believe in the biblical teaching of the new birth, I had simply ceased preaching it or promoting it. The denomination that I was then a part of, simply did not view the "born again" message as being appropriate to the contemporary mindset; it was no longer "politically correct" to preach such beliefs. I had bought into the social gospel mentality "hook, line and sinker."

Although personally I enjoyed the certain knowledge of an eternal hope, I had slowly drifted away from the evangelistic fervor of preaching it. I had gradually moved into the liberal and institutional mindset that dismissed the clear biblical necessity of leading others into that same kind of personal relationship with Christ. I had bought into the doctrinal and ecclesiastical traditions which relegated the new birth experience to the outmoded beliefs of the fanatical fringe. All that was necessary was to baptize the children, send them to confirmation class, encourage them to attend church and hope for the best. It was felt that preaching the "born again" experience would be needlessly uncomfortable to persons in the pew and could even be hazardous to my ministry career. Not only had I not personally witnessed to Kenneth about a personal relationship with Christ, I hadn't even spoken of it in my preaching. My ministry had taken on the carnal and institutional attitudes of religion, while matters of the Spirit were forced to reside in the back recesses of my mind or interest.

The urgency of my own failure to prepare people for life or eternity began to weigh upon my conscience. My preaching had become a watered-down version of the Gospel message. My greatest desire was to make everybody feel good about themselves and keep everybody happy but oblivious to their eternal need. My preaching along with my personal life had lost their spiritual and prophetic edge; I had lost my moral compass and biblical reference point. In some of my most courageous moments, I allowed myself to consider my responsibility in regard to the several years of spiritual neglect. It slowly became a question of personal and ministerial accountability. The actuality that I would be held partially responsible for the eternal destiny of those that I had failed began to trouble my mind. The reality of that negligence proved to be the true source of my emotional trauma and spiritual discomfort. My failure by withholding the salvation message had gone hidden beneath the surface of my conscious mind for years but that voice of guilt and conviction was now too laud and intrusive to ignore. The Spirit was attempting to arrest my attention and redirect my focus even though I had learned overtime how to dull the sharp edge of conscience.

I had started out so well but somewhere had allowed myself to get sidetracked. What had happened? Where had I gone so far astray in my spiritual journey? For those first several years when I started preaching, my love for God and His Word was apparent. My passion for preaching and for people had been so intense. I had once been relentless in my pursuit of Christ and His will for my life. In my earliest years in high school, many pastors were gracious enough to allow a young novice to preach in their pulpit and I relished every opportunity afforded to me. During those days my fervor and desire to preach was really evident. Back home on the farm that passion was so great that I would often preach to the cows as they passed in single file toward the milking barn; one of the benefits of growing up in rural America. The cows weren't the best audience to hone my skills but I wasn't choosy and they never complained. Actually, their cool indifference prepared me for any callousness or indifference I might confront among the saints. My life and preaching had been alive in the Spirit as fully as I could understand, and as much as my age and experience would allow.

If opportunities to preach slowed down in the churches or if the cows became too weary of my eager and ranting exhortations, I would go on Sunday afternoons and hold services in one of the local nursing homes. What a sight that was; an eighteen year old boy, trying to preach to a group of senior citizens. But they didn't seem to mind and were really quite attentive; I loved holding services with them and it helped to fill their lonely hours, so we were a happy match. Although they were all too wise for my adolescent ramblings they were polite enough to listen. Few were as alert or as enthusiastic as I would have liked but at least they were a human audience. For some of those dear folks services simply provided some diversion from their normal routine; for others it gave them a break from the loneliness of their rooms; for still others it allowed for an alternate location for their afternoon nap. None of that mattered much to me for it gave me yet another chance to preach and minister to people. I loved the Word and tried to be as sensitive to the Spirit as possible, in spite of my limited understanding and maturity.

After going to that nursing home for a year, I announced to them that I was leaving the following week for college. Those dear saints took up an offering for the ministry that I had provided. I believe the offering was less than three dollars, but their gift was a generosity I shall never forget. In retrospect, I believe that their sacrificial offering was of greater value than that entire year's worth of sermons. I'm sure I had been overpaid. For all that I had gained emotionally from that captive audience, I had gained far more than I had given. The chance to preach and minister to those dear people was of greater worth to me than could be estimated. I'm not sure how much good my boyish efforts furthered them in their spiritual journey, but their graciousness in just being there has never ceased being an encouragement to my spiritual pilgrimage.

I maintained that same devotion to God and His call on my life throughout my years of college. During those years my personal desire to please God allowed the Spirit of God to prevail in the human struggle, meaning my flesh was on the run or at least was not gaining new territory. In the confrontation between the Spirit and the flesh, my carnal self was usually left bloodied upon the field of battle for, at that time in my life, the Spirit was being allowed to lead the charge. My heart and will were strong toward God, His Word and even toward His Holy Spirit, or at least as much as my earlier training allowed. But several years later, my moral and spiritual convictions had gone into retreat and in some situations had been chased from the field. My professional future and denominational attachment had taken front and center ground in my life and ministry. Lesser loyalties had been invited in, to suppress the higher convictions that had once kept me vibrant in the Lord.

After being involved in full time ministry for several years, that former passion for God and His Word seemed only a distant memory. The worst part was that I realized I was spiritually empty within and therefore had no reserves to assist others. The flame was burning low in my own spirit, so low in fact that my passion for God had become more of a smoldering heap than a flaming fire. The spiritual embers barely gave off any heat and even less light. To use another biblical figure of speech, the stream of living water was barely trickling and was well on its way to becoming a stagnate pool. How did I get so far away from God so fast? How had the passion of the Spirit dissipated so quickly? It was almost as if it had departed without my conscious realization. Why hadn't my convictions and compassion protested more loudly? This recognition of my spiritual downward spiral didn't come all at once. God had been trying to get my attention for several years, but I had kept turning a deaf ear to His voice. It was hard to hear the gentle whispers of the Spirit when my then demanding flesh was so vocal, so alluring, so attractive, so pleasant and so much easier.

It had been a year earlier when God made His first attempt to draw me back into the fold and under the wing of His intended will, but I had managed to suppress His every attempt to get through to me. In that same former church where Kenneth (the church member who had died) was a member, there had been another man and family that I felt I had pastorally failed. He was a young farmer and family man named D.J. This young man had fallen from his barn and was rushed to the hospital with a broken back. He was severely injured and his future uncertain. I did my best to perform my pastoral and professional duties of visiting with him and praying my rather innocuous prayers of encouragement. He appreciated my visits and always thanked me, but he and I both knew that neither my presence nor my prayers did much to help or even encourage him.

When I entered his hospital room I was struck by the sight of His predicament. He was suspended in a total body-cast held and controlled by levers and ropes with little allowance for movement. Any unforeseen emergency, medical complication or inappropriate movement, could have resulted in his death. I was so distracted by D. J.'s physical situation that I gave no thought to his soul or spiritual condition. I empathized with his unfortunate and traumatic circumstances, but offered him little hope and even less real spiritual help. You can imagine my embarrassment when I came into his hospital room the following day and found D.J. beaming with excitement and smiling from ear to ear. What a contrast his situation represented; here he was, totally restricted physically by a full body cast, stretched out as if on a torture rack and unable to move for fear of further damage, but he was rejoicing, grinning and emotionally exuberant. I was bewildered, stunned and genuinely surprised at his joyous attitude in the midst of his dire situation.

What had happened to cause such a contradiction between his physical predicament and his overwhelming enthusiasm? The contrast was breath-taking; my unspoken question to myself was, how could this be? D. J. immediately began to tell me about a visit he had received from another pastor from our community who was known for his evangelical fervor. This pastor unashamedly talked to D. J. about his need for salvation. This pastor persisted even after finding out that D.J. was a member of my church. Following a short time of visiting with D.J., the pastor proceeded to pray with him for his situation but also led him in a prayer of repentance and acceptance of Christ as his personal Savior. That prayer of commitment to Christ for personal salvation really worked, for I found myself looking into the eyes of a newly redeemed person and hearing the excitement in the voice of a new creature in Christ Jesus. D.J. had always been a likeable and seemingly good person, but now he was clearly a born again man with a new sense of eternal purpose and destiny.

I rejoiced with D.J. over his new found relationship with the Lord because I remembered my own dramatic conversion many years before. However, I was secretly ashamed that another pastor had to be the one to speak that clear word of witness to him. I was happy for D. J., but I was personally embarrassed, for I knew that I had failed terribly in my own spiritual responsibility to him. I had never individually witnessed to D.J., and what was worse, I had never preached the necessity of a personal relationship with Christ from the pulpit. The reality of my spiritual indiscretion was too obvious for me to ignore. Another minister's faithfulness filled in the gap for D. J.'s spiritual life. I would have been angry with the other pastor for intruding into another shepherd's flock, but I knew that he had been the faithful shepherd to lead a lost lamb to God, and I had been the negligent hireling. I was the unfaithful shepherd who had not only failed to lead the lamb safely into the fold, but had even allowed the thief free access to the flock.

For a few weeks the guilt of my sin of omission stayed with me, but time and increased pastoral activities soon allowed the memory of failure to fade. But now, a year later, I was faced again with my failure to minister life and eternal hope. Kenneth represented now a second case of my spiritual negligence, and this time my spiritual ineptness was too apparent for me to ignore. I had not discharged the privilege of my own faith or the duty of my own high calling. The seriousness of my lack began to take on eternal consequences. I had personally failed at least two church members and God only knew how many eternal destinies I had affected by my disregard for the biblical truth of personal salvation. At least one of my church members had been pulled from the fire of everlasting damnation by another pastor and a second had died with no apparent certainty of his eternal reward.

The enormity of my failed preaching and practice began to weigh heavily upon my own faith and ministry. The load of guilt along with my own spiritual dissatisfaction led me into a time of repentance and a renewed search for personal revival. During those several years it seemed as if the battle-line kept moving back and forth. In the early years the Spirit had proven triumphant over the my flesh and both my life and preaching reflected that fact. After buying into liberal theology, secular philosophy and the higher critical hermeneutic, my life in the Spirit was removed from the field of conflict. The principles of flesh and the spirit of the world were steadily advancing and had taken the high ground. My own sense of spiritual destitution led me to ponder if there might be a realm of Spirit-empowerment that could better equip me for faith and ministry. Because I began to renew my search for God along with seeking the fullness of Christ, God would hear the cry of my heart and lead me into areas of a new exploration of the things of the Spirit, but then that's another story.

AN EXPOSITIONAL INQUIRY INTO THE TEXT

Gal. 5:16-17; Rom. 8:16-17; John 3:16

All of the passages related to our title and text, represent the persistent warfare between flesh and Spirit. The passage in Galatians 5:16-17 expresses Paul's challenging of the saints to make their faith journey a Spirit walk. If we walk in the Spirit, we won't have to be worried about becoming sidetracked and fall into the quagmire of the flesh. Walk in the straight path and you won't get caught in the dangerous quicksand traps or the muddy side marshes of the enemy. In this passage, Paul sets forth the common scrimmages that take place between the flesh and Spirit. The flesh works against the Spirit and the Spirit resists the works of the flesh. They are polar opposites when it comes to their distinct purposes. No truer words could have been stated to represent my own spiritual dilemma. There could not have been a more accurate assessment of my condition. Christ was attempting to draw me closer into the realm of His Spirit, but the flesh maintained its beckoning call. Both attractions compete for the human heart so we are left to choose the object of our desire.

Paul gives us his extended theological perspective on the armed combat that continues even within redeemed persons. Romans 8 is the chapter that best delineates the continuing carnality of the flesh and the intervening liberation of the Spirit. In Romans 8:1-9, Paul boldly declares the believer's new power arises out of his/her new position of being "in Christ Jesus" (Rom. 8:1). However, that new placement in Christ demands a continued decision to walk according to the Spirit's enablement and the Word's expectations. The flesh will continue to stake its claims upon us, but it no longer has judicial rights over us. The flesh has only the ability to influence our actions but can no longer determine our choices or our destinies. Of course, the Spirit's personal work within and upon us, is possible only because of Christ's effectual work through His incarnation, death, resurrection and ascended glory.

The law was involved in the human fiasco of corruption since it acknowledged the righteous claims of God, but had no innate capability to enable its requirements. By Christ's redemptive work and the Spirit's empowering, the impact of the flesh has only the force that we allow it to have. Before the believer was in Christ, he/she was obligated, even bullied to yield to the dictates of the flesh. The flesh functioned in its full strength and could actually determine a person's actions because of the sin principle still operating from within. Mankind without Christ was like a puppet on a string directed by the whims of the flesh, the allurements of the world and the trickery of the devil. Persons had no power to resist this overwhelming pull and were constantly at the mercy of evil's rule. But thanks be to God and His plan of salvation through Christ, our flesh has only the energy to influence our will, but not the power to compel it (Rom.8:2-4).

It is only right that our human mind be involved in both the debilitation and the liberation processes of human existence. According to verses 6-7 found in Romans 8, there is the mind of flesh and the mind of the Spirit. Every person has the flesh mind which is composed of a physical brain with all of its cells, tissues and connectors and a moral inclination because of conscience. For the unbeliever those two parts reflect the sum total of human life, representative as body and soul, for the person's spirit has been made inoperable through sin. As a product of Adam's fall, the normal functioning of our body and soul are totally at the mercy of our unregenerate and fallen capacity.

The true believer has, on the other hand, Christ's indwelling presence which gives one access to the enabling of the Holy Spirit to fulfill the will of God. It is this writer's belief that only the born again person is able to function in the full triune nature of his/her original creation. The believer's new order of life is the result of Christ, of whom Paul says, "The last Adam became a life-giving spirit" (1 Co. 15:45). Only in Christ does our spirit nature become alive again. Herein is the essential component of God's image and Divine likeness in us (Gen. 2:7). This differential reveals the foundation for the deceptive and corruptive view of Eastern Religions and their understanding of human nature or their doctrine of man. These false religions teach that man is a duality of physical matter (body) and divine nature (soul). The interesting thing to note is that their view of mankind describes human nature in its fallen state, but lacking the truth of God's Word they cannot envision the reality of a revived or reborn spirit nature. The deeply disturbing reality about their belief system is that they have no knowledge of, or hope for, the restored human spirit which is the only true link to an awareness of the True and Living God of the Bible. Their alternative is to rely on counterfeit forms of meditation such as yoga or other Eastern methods of achieving god-consciousness which are totally alien to the Scriptures.

Romans 8:7-8 sets forth not only the antithesis of flesh and Spirit but also their corresponding results. Flesh produces death, the Spirit produces life. As Jesus expressed in John 3:6, flesh gives birth to flesh, but Spirit gives birth to spirit. To put it in modern terms, both flesh and Spirit share a common DNA with their progeny. Since all human beings were created with the substance of flesh, the God-given gift of procreation gives us the co-creative ability to reproduce flesh. However, the unredeemed have no capability for reproducing the life of the Spirit, since sin immediately produced spiritual death in every individual, just as it had in Adam (Gen. 2:17; Rom. 7:17-18). Born-again believers on the other hand, are bearers of the Spirit's fruit and gifts (Gal. 5:22-23). Flesh cannot help but produce death because it contains the principle of armed rebellion against God which can be traced all the way back to the conflict in the Garden (Gen. 3:17-19). The Spirit cannot help but produce life because it contains the principle of Christ's resurrection life and the Spirit's essence (Rom 8:9).

As to the operations of the flesh within our nature, F.F. Bruce explains that, in chapters seven and eight, Paul was referring to three phases of the Christian life: "(a) before the law; (b) under the law; (c) set free from the law in Christ."[1] Paul is not just giving us the story of his own personal pilgrimage, here, but the universal account of every person who has accepted the Gospel message. Chapter eight of the book of Romans is our main focus because it is the believer's spiritual struggle regarding the flesh with which we are concerned. Paul makes it clear that even though we are followers of Christ the flesh is still very much alive. The old Adam nature has been crucified with Christ through repentance and faith, but the desires of the flesh have to be dealt with daily and on a continuing basis. The Christian, in the words of Bruce, " is like a person living simultaneously on two planes, eagerly longing to lead a life in keeping with the higher plane, but sadly aware of the strength of indwelling sin that keeps on pulling him down to the lower plane."[2]

As sons and daughters of the kingdom of God, we enjoy the benefits of the kingdom in the here and now but we live in hope of the fullness of His kingdom yet to come. For this age or season of time, we must live with the tension between the pull of the flesh and the draw of the Spirit and as such we live 'between the times' (Gal. 5:17). In some ways the flesh/Spirit strife is more intense in the believer since his or her new-born spirit establishes a real and vibrant opponent for the flesh. The flesh is no longer the dominant force upon the battleground of man's soul, because it now only has the rule that we allow it. Even with the inward aid of the Spirit, the flesh is still a force with which one must continue to reckon, but the flesh principle no longer has the power to dictate. It is not the tyrant it once was, since there is One greater that is now resident within us (Greater is He 1 John 4:4). Bruce affirms: "Believers are perfect as to their justification, but their sanctification is only begun. It is a progressive work."[3]

Returning to my own situation, I had been given the life of the Holy Spirit through my initial conversion experience, however, I had gotten so caught up in a liberal and unbiblical mind-set that I had embraced a theological position that denied any semblance of spirituality. My witness became nonexistent, my moral life began to go into a decline and my devotional life deteriorated into total neglect. As a result of this, my preaching became an exercise in unimportant theologizing, social moralizing, intellectual philosophizing and a plethora of religious platitudes that left no one morally challenged or spiritually changed. My lifestyle revealed that one can have had a genuine conversion experience, but may still operate at various levels within the flesh/Spirit spectrum. At this point of my personal blurring between flesh and Spirit there remained little or no room for the direction or empowerment of the Spirit.

My preaching reflected the anti-supernatural bias that I had been raised in and trained by. The evangelical perspective I was raised with, instilled in me the idea that the miracles of the Bible were true but that miraculous signs and wonders along with the gifts of the Holy Spirit had ceased with the canonizing of the Bible. My liberal graduate education further eroded any and all acceptance of, or hope for the supernatural works of Christ or the miraculous wonders of the Spirit, either past or present. I was taught in seminary that the Bible was not the Word of God, but only contained the Word of God. In other words the Bible should not be considered as faith's only source or standard of divine truth. I was encouraged to doubt Moses authorship of the Pentateuch, Christ's virgin birth and bodily resurrection and other cardinal tenets of the Bible. It would have been easier for me to acknowledge what I did not believe in, by the time I graduated. In retrospect, one had to wonder what positive message I still retained that was worthy of proclamation. That reality indeed, was my spiritual dilemma, but then that's also another story.

SUPPORTING QUOTES RELATED TO THE TEXT

"Under the old order, before the coming of the Spirit, it was impossible to do the will of God, and if people's lives are still dominated by that old order, to do His will remains an impossibility."[4]

"All that the law required by way of conformity to the will of God is now realized in the lives of those who are controlled by the Holy Spirit and are released from their servitude to the old order. God's commands have now become God's enablings."[5]

"In Paul's view it was precisely the coming of the Spirit which set up the already—not yet tension in the believer's life."[6]

"The already—not yet tension is set up precisely by the fact that the Spirit by His coming begins to reclaim man for God, to contest the sway of man's selfish passions, his self-sufficiency and self-indulgence, and, if man wills, to defeat them."[7]

"Consequently the Spirit's redeeming work has only begun and is necessarily incomplete (Phil. 1:6): for the Spirit has come to take possession of the whole man."[8]

"It is precisely because the dividing line between the two is so difficult to draw that the believer must stand in constant dependence on the Spirit for the charisma of discernment and on his fellow Christians for the charisma of evaluation."[9]

"Thus the antithesis of Paul's anthropology and his Christology find their resolution in his pneumatolgy."[10]

"(Matt.11:4-5)...Jesus wanted John to know, 'I am speaking and things are happening. Change is occurring. There's evidence, not just through my persuasive speech, but there is evidence from heaven that I am who I say I am.'"[11]

"If there is to be a vital Holy Ghost restoration of His people, it will be because God Himself will come down and demonstrate His power in the earth. It will be because men and women yield to God from their innermost beings."[12]

"Today the Pentecostal world is out of balance in its concern and warnings about the misuse of the supernatural."[13]

"The man who, more than anyone in the early Church, has given us his assessment of the factors in evangelism is St.

Luke. And for him the two main ones are the very factors which men do not provide, namely the Spirit of God and the Word of God."[14]

"Preaching, then, whether in synagogue, Christian assembly, or open air, whether normal or under direct inspiration, was a not unimportant factor in the methods of the mission. Nevertheless the break with the synagogue, the rise of persecution and the absence of Christian buildings for worship all hindered formal proclamation of the gospel...However, despite the hazards and the difficulties, great numbers of Christians must have really given themselves to preaching all over the ancient world."[15]

QUESTIONS RELATED TO THE TEXT

1. How much does a solid beginning in our faith guarantee our continuation in the biblical truth that we have been taught?

2. During what I call my liberal years was my eternal salvation affected? What might my personal judgment be from Christ for my former failing to preach and warn others about their lost condition?

3. How much does our culture of unbelief bear a responsibility for the rejection of the whole Gospel?

4. What does our nation's failure to embrace the Gospel of the kingdom say about the purpose and power of preaching?

5. How does Romans chapters 7-8 reflect both our human dilemma of still being in the flesh and our spiritual prospects of living triumphantly by the Spirit?

6. What does my faith pilgrimage vividly confirm about the connection between character and preaching? What does it affirm about the link between the need for the Spirit's presence and preaching's power?

7. How much of our western form of Christianity is, in your view, dominated by the flesh principle rather than that of the Spirit?

CHAPTER FIVE

JOHN 20:22; ACTS 2:4; MARK 16:20

SPIRIT LIFE, EMPOWERMENT AND THE GOSPEL

A NARRATIVE RESPONSE TO THE TEXT

I had preached on the week-ends at several student pastorates in rural to small town churches. I also had pastored churches on a full time basis, ranging from medium size churches in small towns to larger churches in medium size towns. Linda and I were then looking forward to pastoral ministry in the small town of Auburn, Illinois, just a few miles from Springfield, the capital of the State. The church had been 450 members and at one time its attendance reflected its membership, but the average attendance had dwinded to about 50 for the Sunday morning service. There was much to do and a lot of work lay ahead of us but Auburn offered a great opportunity. I was excited as my new preaching assignment awaited me with all its possibilities and challenges.

We had been offered several options but we were excited about this church's potential for numerical growth. The congregation seemed to feel that the greatest need was for good pulpit speaking with polished oratory. I had been working on improving my homiletic skills for several years and felt myself ready for just such a challenge. I believed I was up to the task and gladly accepted the challenge of displaying my homiletic expertise to a church that represented a good mix of professionals, blue collar workers and well-to-do farmers. Linda had been able to immediately secure a teaching job in the local elementary school which gave us a second income. Angie and Ami, our two daughters, were blessed to grow up receiving the nurturing of a loving community. They were able to experience the benefits of growing up in the honored and respected environment of one of the historic denominations, with all its benefits and immediate community acceptance.

I was exactly where I wanted to be. I was enjoying the position, prestige, popularity and the power of being a religious leader and minister in small town America. The honing of my preaching skills was paying off. The older members were returning to the church and new families were coming out to join in the new enthusiasm that was spreading throughout the area. Former members and new people were coming to hear a lively and well prepared sermon and to enjoy the fellowship and the growing neighborhood excitement. The folks seemed to like what they were being fed, even though I knew that any well constructed speech would have sufficed, regardless of the biblical content. Having come from an evangelical background I realized that preaching should at least give the impression of being based on the Bible, however. Therefore I worked hard to give the correct appearance of being both professional and contemporary in every area, but especially with respect to my Sunday morning sermon.

I took consolation and encouragement from my weekly routine and discipline for sermon preparation. I even attended the Marble Collegiate Church in New York City and observed Norman Vincent Peale's method of motivational preaching. I was fascinated by his approach and developed a similar oratory style of preaching without standing behind the pulpit and without notes, just as he did. His style worked for him and it seemed to be working for me, adding to my popularity as a community speaker and a pulpit preacher. I felt that I had climbed yet another rung on the ladder of ministerial development and ecclesiastical success. To be honest though during this same period, I could note my hunger for more than just material, vocational and numerical growth. The contradiction between my ministerial success and my spiritual anxiety only increased with every one of my professional achievements.

Linda and I were right in the middle of moving into our new parsonage when we were visited by the young man who filled the role of lay leader in the church. In fact, Ron and his wife Marcia helped us carry our furniture from the moving van into our new home. They were amiable, young, energetic, professional and positive minded people; I was impressed with them both on several levels. While I was impacted by them in regard to their outgoing and committed witness, it was also on this particular front that they concerned me; I was both cautious of, and not a little reluctant about, the force and vibrancy of their testimonies. Frankly, I had not met anyone quite like Ron and Marcia and that disquieted me to some degree. They seemed to be overly devoted to their beliefs and just a bit overboard in their enthusiasm and constant talk about Jesus. Actually I thought they talked far too much about both Jesus and the Holy Spirit. Their first name familiarity with Christ was tolerable, but the constant references to the Holy Spirit, was definitely outside my comfort zone. Yet, I was consciously moved by their spirit and their passion for the Lord, a reminder no doubt of my own spiritual emptiness and longing to return to their kind of close relationship with the Lord.

Within a short time, Ron and Marcia came to share the basis of their excitement for Christ and His Word. They were disarmingly forthright yet not pushy in their testimony about their conversion to Christ and their Baptism in the Holy Spirit. I could be respectful of their message until they announced that they both had received the gift of speaking in other tongues. That was all I needed to hear since I recognized that the term speaking in tongues' was a phrase that carried so many negative connotations from my past. That term "speaking in tongues" made me cringe and caused me to put up everyone of my protective mechanisms. My first thought was,

"I knew there had to be something wrong with these people." They were confirming what I had wanted to believe, that they were after all "just too weird!" I began to do all I could to keep my distance from them without being too obvious.

After all, I had grown up being warned about folks like Ron and Marcia. I had been cautioned about 'people like them' all my life, having heard criticisms about 'those people' from Sunday school teachers, many pastors and from other believers that I had greatly respected. I had heard many negative remarks throughout my college days from both students and teachers; several classmates and I made jokes and mocked such Pentecostal beliefs during my seminary days. I well remembered a group of us attending a Pentecostal revival service to poke fun, all in the name of academic openness and educational experience. I decided fairly quickly that Ron and Marcia were a couple I had to tolerate but I definitely was not interested in getting chummy with. My fear, prejudice and lack of understanding put an emotional damper on our fellowship though I tried very hard not to show it by my behavior. However since Ron's position was lay leader in the church, I knew I had to at least act cordial toward him.

Deep within me, I knew great inner turmoil because I wanted what Ron and Marcia had, but I didn't want to follow their path to receiving it. One could say, I liked the product but I wasn't fond of the packaging. There had to be another way to experiencing their joy, commitment and renewal without what I perceived as being the excesses, the hype and the so called present-day gifts of the Holy Spirit, especially the emphasis on tongues. At the core of my dilemma was the question of how to proceed since I felt that I needed to maintain an intellectual openness to all possibilities without giving in to what I considered their 'great error' and hyperspirituality.

I desperately wanted more of Christ's presence and power in my life, but was still not sure about the connection between Holy Spirit Baptism and tongues. Intellectually I believed in the Holy

Spirit as the third person of the Trinity, but I wasn't sure I wanted Him to have any further access beyond my intellect. I wanted more of His presence, but was more at home with His distance. Theologically, I had nothing against the person or work of the Holy Spirit. My reluctance concerned more of what I deemed as those uncommon, inconvenient and mostly interruptive acts that were so often associated with His presence. Certainly I did not want anyone interrupting what I had worked so hard to accomplish, not even the Holy Spirit. Since I saw my career agenda as intact, on track and as my professional plans were unfolding nicely, any radical adjustments might jeopardize my future strategies.

I was concerned that all their talk about experiencing the Holy Spirit might be implying an experiential inadequacy in me. Their words and actions puzzled me; was it a game of spiritual 'one-ups-man-ship', or was it perhaps an attempt to upstage or even usurp my leadership? Their undeniable sincerity and inexhaustible faithfulness to the work of the church forced me to focus on my own spiritual relationship with God. Over time it finally occurred to me that the answers to my quandary did not lay in obsessing about their experiences or my lack of experiences. It was more about developing and strengthening my own relationship with Christ as Lord of my whole being. I realized that the source of my need was a clearer grasp of these spiritual realities, but I also recognized that such clarity would come from the source I had too long neglected, namely the Bible as the Word of God. I knew that the insight and understanding I desired would not come from the scholarly commentaries, theological texts, or philosophical systems that I had grown accustomed to relying upon, but from the Bible alone.

I was by then becoming all too aware of the liberal education that had diminished my love for the Bible and had resulted in a spiritual dryness, even though it purported to honor Scripture through the historical-critical method of study. In the name of intellectual honesty, hermeneutical accuracy and academic excellence I had come close to losing my faith in the name of faith. On the other side of that recognition there was still the memory of a love for God's Word that I could never quite erase from my consciousness. That remembering was like a long lost love that yearned to be rekindled, therefore I set out on a quest to search the Bible as God's Word for the answers to my many questions, and temporarily laid aside my focus on having an experience. What began in part as a research project to prove that I could experience the fullness of the Spirit my way, turned out to be Christ's recovery program for a renewed life in the Spirit by experiencing it in His way.

For almost a year I researched and studied the relationship between experiencing Christ and the Holy Spirit. Intentionally and intensely I probed the questions surrounding my own early conversion, my call into the ministry, why I still sensed such spiritual inadequacy and what the Spirit's role should be in my present life and ministry. The overarching issue seemed to be focused on how much weight, if any, should be given to the manifestation of the Spirit's gifts today? And, of course, that opened the whole debate about the place of tongues in relationship to both Christ and the Holy Spirit as paramount in my thinking. It took awhile, in fact quite awhile, but slowly answers began to emerge along the lines of three major questions. (1) Was the experience of tongues an important issue in the Bible? (2) Was the subject of speaking in tongues a matter of importance for the church age, especially after the era of the Apostles and the canonization of the Bible? (3) If tongues was of experiential value, in what way was it significant for my life and ministry and did I really need it? After many months of inquiry, study and meditating on those questions, my answer to all three was a resounding "yes." Only over time have I come to realize the legitimacy of my quest, in that I most needed first to discover the validity of tongues as a biblical mandate and only after that as a spiritual experience.

Having come to the belief that speaking in tongues was definitely in God's Word, that it was a biblical experience for today and that I genuinely needed the Spirit's empowering blessing, I began ardently to seek Baptism in the Holy Spirit with the evidence of speaking in other tongues, just as the Bible seemed to affirm. It was important to me that I was not just seeking an experience for the sake of having an experience. Any such experience needed to cohere to Scriptural requirements and with power to correspond to Christ's mandate for fulfilling His kingdom and His missional purpose for the Church. There were many questions yet to be answered, but I had definitely reached the point of personal readiness for whatever God wanted to do in my life.

Realizing that any experience of God or of the Spirit should always be assimilated into a lifestyle of both Christ-like character and Christ-like ministry, the cry of our heart must first and foremost be a desire for more of Christ than the longing for an experience. I was also discerning a mentality that had been prevalent in so much of the religious mindset that I had grown up observing. Much of my church life and theological training was so suspicious of the experiential dimension of faith that I had come to distrust anything that I couldn't mentally grasp or rationally understand. Reason and intellect dominated almost every aspect of my life and ministry. There was little room in my version of faith for human emotion and spiritual passion. My own personal and public style of worship was inhibited and restrained and based, not on Scripture but on custom, tradition and cultural preference. I came to realize the inadequacies of this mental attitude simply from the fresh reading of the Bible and not just through personal experiences. Yet I have come to understand that there can be no growth in Christ or depth of understanding His Word outside of ongoing and consistent personal experiencing of the Spirit.

I was now ready for more of Him than my previous views had either acknowledged or envisioned. I began to actively seek others who might share more fully with me in regard to these concerns and where I might go to experience this 'phenomena' personally. I was neither shy about my search nor intimidated by former warnings. I was a preacher on a mission; I was excited about discovering for myself what I had come to believe was biblical, appropriate and for me essential. Immediately upon arriving at my decision, Ron told me about a ministry couple who was coming to the city of Springfield, Illinois to teach about Baptism in the Holy Spirit. This couple was known as the 'Happy Hunters' and well-known as charismatic teachers whose background was one of the other major historic denominations. My sense of focus and determination was shocking, even to myself. This kind of boldness and adventure was foreign to my personality and demeanor yet I was totally convinced of the rightness and validity of my quest.

Without fanfare or consideration of the challenge ahead, when the day of the meeting arrived I journeyed to the Springfield Grant Hotel and listened intently to what the Hunters shared and taught. At the end of their presentation, they gave a subdued but forthright invitation for those seeking salvation and the Baptism in the Holy Spirit. Even though the audience was primarily made of ministers and it might sound strange that they gave an invitation to salvation, I personally knew ministers in several of the mainline churches that had never experienced a personal relationship with Christ. They were taught in their denominations to rely upon the rituals and traditions of their church's doctrines and policies and therefore had laid no claim to being born again or to having had any personal encounter with the Lord.

When the Hunters gave the invitation for the Baptism of the Holy Spirit, I was one of the first to reach the altar to accept their offer. I was very much surprised at who I saw standing around me, to both pray for and be prayed for. There were many at the altar. It was a group composed of a wonderful diversity of Protestant and Catholic ministers each praying for a special touch from God for both personal Baptism in the Spirit and for spiritual renewal in general. I had never seen such an ecumenical convergence of denominational seekers. I had witnessed and participated in several ecumenical gatherings, but they were always humanly programmed and felt strategically contrived. This was different! All those gathered there seemed compelled by a common desire to seek the fullness of Christ's blessing and impartation of the Holy Spirit. As several prayed for me I was expectant that Christ would immerse me in His empowering presence, not because I was deserving of it, but because I was truly desiring all that belonged to every believer in Christ.

Nothing was demanded, forced or manipulated, but after only a short time of praying and inviting more of Jesus and the Holy Spirit into my life, I heard myself speaking a new language. It was not the highly charged emotional experience I had expected, yet the very fact that I was speaking what sounded like a fluent language I had never learned was evidence enough that God had fulfilled His biblical promise. I had been led to think that these tongue speakers went off into emotional frenzies, lapsed into glassy-eyed trances and were manipulated into wild and ecstatic displays. I had to acknowledge that all I saw were people enthusiastically worshiping the Lord and exhibiting a hunger for God that I had never observed. The folks I saw were not glary-eyed, uneducated, downtrodden or over-emotional types. These believers were well groomed, highly trained and appeared totally sane; the only thing they had in common was a weariness of dreary religion, dead ritual, lifeless worship and head doctrines that never seemed to reach the heart.

My experience of receiving the gift of tongues was joyous and gave me a deeper sense of personal connectedness to Christ; it would only be later that I would come to realize the sweeping inward and outward transformation that began in that Friday morning service in the ballroom of an historic downtown hotel. I felt a greater sense of peace and tranquility, but certainly no sense of mystic enrapturing. Even though I knew that I had just experienced something that could only have come from a supernatural source, there was also something about the event that seemed very normal and this-worldly. The language I privately spoke seemed to have all the components of language in general, but also conveyed an intimacy and directness to God that I had never known. I had studied High School French, College Latin and Seminary Greek and Hebrew and I knew quite well that I was not that skilled as a linguist, but this new language had all the tonal expressions of normal language poured forth with the rhythm and force of an unobstructed river (John 7:38).

The most exhilarating aspect of this new means of prayer communication was the opening up of a new understanding of the Bible, a greater awareness of the person of Jesus, a fresh significance of both the Holy Spirit's assisting in character formation and increased ministry effectiveness. I was convinced that what I had received was of God and I was prepared to move on with a quiet confidence that God would both direct and sustain me throughout whatever lay ahead. I knew that in some ways it was a new beginning, but in other ways it was like the recapturing of old territory that the enemies' occupation force had robbed me of, by subtle trickery and deliberate misinformation.

I knew the Lord was pleased and I knew that I had been blessed, but now I had another difficulty to face. This obstacle was not insurmountable, but it was still a situation I had to face namely; how to explain the events of the day to my wife, Linda. My plan seemed simple enough; say nothing and act as if nothing had happened, just remain cool, calm and collected. I would speak only when spoken to and respond with brief answers to direct questions and pray for the opportune and most inoffensive moment to share more.

Without my even telling her the whole story, let me just comment that as I shared with her my experience, she was fearful that I had really gone off the deep-end this time. In wisdom, and despite her personal consternation, Linda decided to hold off judgment and wait to see if my new experience made any real difference in me. Initially our life together was a little tense. She was quietly kind and allowed me time and space to work out my own spiritual path and journey. Also, I knew that I had plenty of work for the Spirit to do in me without adding worry about her condition; I remained content to allow the Spirit to do His own work in my wife with as little interference from me as possible. This mutual but unilateral procedure continued over the next several months, which actually proved to be the most conductive atmosphere for the Spirit to accomplish His most effective work in both of us. We both gingerly navigated around one another by a sort of unarmed and undeclared truce, proving mutually advantageous for peace on the home front.

To express the situation in only slightly exaggerated terms, in Linda's mind I had crossed over behind enemy lines, gotten captured, been severely tortured, interrogated and brainwashed and then released back into the population. In her words, "It's now you and them against me." She was right to question my former spiritual choices and resulting theological instability, since I was the one that had been ensnared by the corruptive liberal message. In spite of her appropriate concerns, she and I tried hard to be patient with each other, even though we were both faced with an entirely new dimension and reality that had significantly changed our lives. For the time being I was content to allow the Spirit to convict and prompt change in several of my own sinful actions and attitudes, while Linda was also allowing the Lord to convince and direct her toward a greater understanding of the Holy Spirit's work. There were many new aspects to work through, but in a very short period of time, the Spirit would lead her into a most amazing journey of her own, but then that's another story.

AN EXPOSITIONAL INQUIRY INTO THE TEXT
John 20:22; Acts 2:4; Mark 16:20

In John 20:22, Jesus breathed upon the disciples and they received the life of the Spirit, which was also an initial work of the resurrected Lord. This was their moment of conversion or their experience of being born-again in the biblical sense. This beginning work of salvation in those disciples was the initiating work of Christ and the Spirit for God's new creation miracle in the lives of those earliest believers. Thanks to John's incorporating of this particular moment into his text, the dynamic of the resurrected Lord is tied to the work of the Holy Spirit. Also the Spirit's historical past and present are inextricably linked with the Spirit's work in the *Eschaton,* connecting the disciples' new life in Christ, the fresh empowerment to follow, and their future hope at the resurrection of the dead in Christ.

Just as surely as the pre-incarnated Christ breathed the breath of His Spirit-life into the first man, He was here breathing His resurrection life into the disciples. This is why born-again believers cherish Paul's reference to our being God's new creation (2 Co. 5:17). Also Paul's referring to Christ as a life-giving Spirit (1 Co.15:45b) makes a scriptural connection to this resurrection scene. This passage in John 20 also points backward in time to mankind's creation in Genesis, where Christ first breathed His Spirit-life into Adam. It is surprising to me that several important scholars view this key verse as problematic rather than seeing it as a clarifying text to help in interpreting the work of the risen Christ and that of the Spirit. This verse is both preceded and followed by verses that join together Christ's work, the Spirit's missionary commissioning and the Church's charismatic authority. In regards to God's work of re-creation within the human race, this verse is crucial.

When these Jewish apostles wrote and spoke of the work of the Spirit, they did so in terms of their own heritage. The words for spirit in both the Hebrew (*ruah*) and the Greek (*pneuma*) often refer to breath. William Barclay affirms: "*Breath is life; and therefore the promise of the Spirit is the promise of life. The Spirit of God breathes God's life into human beings.*"[1] This encounter between Jesus and the disciples is definitely about the life of the Spirit within the believer. This experience for the disciples was as climactic for the new order of creation as was God's creating of the first Adam in the old order of creation. Just as the first man became a living soul in the old creation, the disciples also became living souls in the new creation implying the reviving of their spirit nature within them. This New Testament reality of the Holy Spirit's life-giving presence is also pictured in the Old Testament story of Ezekiel and God's breathing new life into dry bones (Ezek. 37:5).

Like the disciples of old, all persons need to first have their spirit-life restored, before anything else can spiritually take place in their soul-life. Genuine conversion returns a person to his/her true triune nature that existed before the human fall (Gen. 2:7). In relationship to our own individual innocence before partaking of the old Adamic nature, we all still shared that triune nature. When sin entered in, we were all reduced to function with the duel nature of body and soul, which meant our human existence without a human living spirit (Gen. 2:17; 1 Co. 15:48; Rom. 5:12). The triune nature still exists potentially within, but the true essence of that triune nature is no longer operational, at least as long as we remain under the old fallen order. With our new birth by the Spirit however, our spirit person came back to life (John 3:3) and our spirit begins to vibrate once more and pulsate with new creation life. For that reason man is not true man, unless or until he partakes of the new manhood or personhood in Christ. This verse in John 20 is therefore John's account of the disciples' new birth experience with its corresponding reality of eternal life.

A complementary verse in John's Gospel relating to spirit-life records Jesus saying, "It is the Spirit who gives life; the flesh profits nothing. The words that I speak to you are spirit, and they are life." (John 6:63). About this verse, Merrill C. Tenney comments that "the cumulative emphasis of 'spirit' is on the supernatural aspect of human life."[2] The value of John 6:63 with John 20:22 reveal the linkage between Jesus as the incarnated Word, the words of the gospel message, the resurrected Christ and the work of the Spirit.

We begin to see a beautiful cohesion among all the New Testament books, in regard to the person and work of the Spirit. The verses in John 20:21-23 bring together Christ's ministry, the Spirit's new creation life and the Church's charismatic authority for worship, wonders and witness.

As I previously mentioned, it is unfortunate that some biblical scholars tend to see this passage in problematic terms rather than viewing it as one of the great interpretive passages to the entire Gospel account. Each book of the New Testament expresses its own unique quality in view of Christ's message and work, but their inexorable unity and continuity are without parallel. John is here acknowledging that Christ's person and work and the Spirit's person and work cannot be separated without destroying the very fabric of the Gospel. Just as the feasts of Passover and Pentecost each represent distinct historical events, they cannot be separated theologically. The reception of the Spirit's life must precede the giving of the Spirit's power.

In Luke 11:20 Jesus declares, "But if I cast out demons with the finger of God, surely the kingdom of God has come upon you." In the thought of James D. G. Dunn, that present manifestation of the eschatological kingdom was present in Jesus mainly because of the presence of the eschatological Spirit.[3] In regard to this verse, Dunn notes: "In other words, it was not so much a case of 'Where I am there is the kingdom', as, 'Where the Spirit is there is the kingdom.'"[4] In Christological terms, Jesus embodied the prophetic Son of Man and the miracle-working son of God. It is by the Spirit that Jesus alone can draw together both titles and themes and therefore He is the only One who can usher in the *Eschaton* or the age to come.

In Jesus, the disciples beheld the present demonstrations of this future kingdom. His preaching and miracles during His ministry were sufficient evidence, but His resurrection was ultimate proof that He was indeed the eschatological and charismatic Man of the Spirit. Jesus' Spirit anointed preaching and His Spirit empowered wonders were displays that God's future kingdom was already upon them. Only one final epoch of the Spirit was yet to be realized. For God's kingdom purposes to be fulfilled historically, a new community of faith needed to be created as the instrument of this same eschatological and charismatic Spirit. It was precisely that needed mandate that brings us to the Day of Pentecost.

Acts 2:4 gives us the historical account of the Spirit's birthing of the Church, Christ's community of faith. This fellowship of believers was to be made up of persons who would individually be endowed with the power of the Spirit, just as they had been imputed with the life of the Spirit. Although some early believers had been living out many of the aspects of a new community such as fellowship, worship and prayer, they must have sensed that there was more to come. Jesus Himself had thoroughly explained it all (John 16:7-14; 7:37-39), but explanation without experience is never adequate for fully knowing a truth. Just as the Spirit had formerly made Himself known with His gentle breath of new Spirit-life, now He would become known by the force of mighty wind for Spirit-empowered witness; same Spirit, different dimension of His presence. Both are available and essential for believers and the Church to function in fullness. The work of both new life and new power are the two experiential sides of a single coin of currency exchange.

I have always appreciated my own evangelical foundation and I still recognize the important contribution of the Evangelical Church for its biblical witness and missionary fervor. It is however, not difficult to understand its unfortunate limitation when it comes to accomplishing a total global mission and declaration of the Gospel of the kingdom. Even though Evangelicals share a portion of common history with Pentecostals, the former group's reading of Acts 2 is always quite predictable, unfortunate and incomplete. Their commentaries are useful and contain many excellent insights, but fail to encourage believers to seek all that belongs to them. As long as believers seek God's fullness but demand having it on their own terms, they never quite measure up to the biblical norm or dynamic pattern that we see in the early Church. For example, after denying the continuing reality of speaking in tongues or moving in the power of spiritual gifts many Evangelicals are frustrated because their effectiveness in witness does not correspond to the biblical experience of empowerment. For example one author realizes that the scene of Pentecost "describes what a biblical church really looks like, not only in the first century, but in every century from the Lord's ascension until his second coming."[5] Many have a continuing longing to regain what has been lost, yet are unwilling to appropriate Christ's intended means of retrieving the goal.

The above quote in regard to what the Church should look like, is a verbal contradiction if the Church continues to reject the real Pentecostal pattern. The anti-supernatural bias that exists in so much of the Western Church today is legitimate only if the original purpose of the Church was simply to carry on the structural forms of organization, minus its pneumatic empowerment and charismatic responsibility. If the Church fails to reflect the Pentecostal church model, it neglects both the charismatic nature of the Church and dismisses the charismatic nature of the resurrected Christ. As long as any portion of the community of faith demeans this component of its biblical legacy, that segment of the Church will not, nor indeed cannot move in its God-given authority and power. Christ's vision for a Church that moves in all His available power and energy will be postponed, as long as believers allow their theological systems to dominate and limit their experience of Christ's fullness. The greatest tragedy for any form of proclaiming the Gospel is that our experience of the Spirit impacts the anointing of the Spirit upon that witness. It is the anointing of the Spirit alone that releases and imparts the supernatural results of all forms of verbal declaration. We have too long settled for a religion of reason instead of a spirituality of the Spirit.

Only after Pentecost did apostolic preaching reflect the eschatological and charismatic character of Jesus. Their preaching was also characterized by prophetic authority and miraculous works. All of this is made clear from our third text found in Mark 16:15-20 where Jesus gives a more detailed version of the Great Commission, one that is Pentecostal from beginning to end. For those who love to deny the validity of Mark's so called longer version, one only has to read the book of Acts to find support for that writer's charismatic and supernatural emphasis. The apostolic preaching and miracle-working ministries of the early Church were as epochal as was Jesus ministry, just as He said it would be (John 14:12); both Jesus and the early Spirit-baptized believers operated from the same energy source as do we.

Sin and sickness was being routed and the war was being waged against Satan through the ministries of those early believers, in the same way they had in Jesus' ministry. When this kind of intimate and dynamic fellowship with the Spirit is missing in the Church of any age, something is tragically awry. In the words of Dunn, "Without this, 'fellowship' (*koivwvia*) lacks all substance; it remains a jargon word or ideal and never becomes an existential reality."[6] Our particular one verse text found in Mark 16:20 is even more pointed when it comes to connecting anointed preaching with resulting supernatural signs and wonders. Mark could not have been clearer when he acknowledged: "And they went out and preached everywhere, the Lord working with them and confirming the word through the accompanying signs."

My story was similar to that of the first disciples. I am persuaded that when I was eleven years old I had a living encounter with the risen Lord, and therefore enjoyed the life of the Spirit, but did not receive Christ's empowering gift until I was baptized in the Holy Spirit (with the evidence of the gift of tongues) at the age of 33. I don't believe that such a gap in the time sequence is necessary, if the Church is doing an effective job of explaining and proclaiming the complete work of the Holy Spirit. Every work of the Spirit is meant to take us from level to level in our faith, but each work represents the many threads of a single cloth that begins with conviction of sin and ends with resurrection or rapture. When can one experience this Spirit-Baptism? This experience is available when the believer's spirit is open and not cluttered by doubt, lack of appreciation, misinformation, defensive posturing, or inordinate fear. The greatest hindrance to the Spirit's Baptism for believers is that of allowing one's traditions to make null and void the Word of God (Mt. 15:6).

SUPPORTING QUOTES RELATED TO THE TEXT

"It means that charismata are indispensable to community, that community is a reality only when it is charismatic community...It means that believers are members of the community only as charismatics; that they are charismatics only as members of the community."[7]

"In Paul's view it was precisely the coming of the Spirit which set up the already-not yet tension in the believer's life. For *the Spirit is the future good which has become present for the man of faith—that power of the not yet has already begun to be realized in his present experience.*"[8]

"From the resurrection appearances stemmed the sense of *obligation* to mission; but only the experiences of Spirit brought the inner *compulsion* to mission and *confirmation* of its widening outreach."[9]

"One of our basic concerns about evangelical hermeneutics in the past is our tendency to adopt a very cognitive, rationalistic model which often misses either the nature of the gospel itself or the dynamic quality of life in the Spirit."[10]

"It would seem from any valid reading of Luke and Paul that the gift of the Spirit was not some sort of adjunct to Christian experience, nor was it some kind of second and more significant part of Christian experience. It was rather the chief element of Christian life, from beginning to end."[11]

"I think it is fair to note that if there is one thing that differentiates the early church from its twentieth-century counterpart it is the level of awareness and experience of the presence and power of the Holy Spirit."[12]

"Today evil profoundly holds the world in its grip, and humans desperately need deliverance through signs and wonders—a deliverance that relates to the way God decisively deals with evil as a result of Jesus' mighty works."[13]

"In other words, Luke is fond of referring to the teaching and healing activities of Jesus. Repeatedly, he includes material referring to both of these activities into what he has obtained from his sources (Luke 5:15, 6:17-19; 9:1-2). While this tendency certainly indicates that proclamation and miracles are complementary, the fact that these references generally occur in the context of a miracle story suggests that Luke is especially concerned to highlight the significance of proclamation."[14]

"As a matter of fact, it is this motif of power that makes Jesus' experience at Jordan the prototype of the Pentecostal effusion of the Spirit upon the infant Church poised on the threshold of its worldwide ministry in Jesus' name, and in the power and demonstration of the Holy Spirit."[15]

"If the book of Acts bears witness to normative Christian experience—and it indubitably does—then, by every biblical standard of measurement, contemporary church-life is subnormal."[16]

QUESTIONS RELATED TO THE TEXT

1. What role has tradition played in your spiritual experience and when might those traditions be either positive or negative?

2. Why may an emphasis on the Holy Spirit result in the neglect of the Father and Son? How might that criticism be a false presupposition or misguided concern?

3. What part does a person's sense of spiritual need play in relationship to the Baptism of the Holy Spirit?

4. We have written much about the Church moving in Pentecostal power today, but how important is it that the Church also operate as an ethical community?

5. How or when is it possible for the Pentecostal Church to fall into the same failures and entrapments as the non-Pentecostal churches when it comes to having low expectations of the preaching event?

6. What may be significant about expecting verbal witnessing in the marketplace to carry the same anointing of the Holy Spirit as pulpit preaching?

CHAPTER SIX

MARK 2:1-3; LUKE 4:43-44; 5:12-17; ISAIAH 6:1-9

PREACHING FOR THE WONDER OF HIS PRESENCE

A NARRATIVE RESPONSE TO THE TEXT

Right in the middle of her sermon, Katherine Kuhlman pointed with her finger to the far right side of the auditorium and in a very matter of fact way declared, "The cloud of the Spirit is here tonight!" My wife Linda heard what this well-known evangelist had just boldly proclaimed and it grabbed her attention. My wife the skeptic thought, "Well, if this lady has the audacity to say such a thing, I want to see it!" While the speaker continued to preach as if nothing unusual had occurred, Linda looked toward the spot where Kuhlman had indicated. Sure enough, exactly as she had announced, there it was! A visible cloud was hanging just above the heads of the people as Kuhlman had declared in a very matter-of-fact way.

It was the summer of 1974. My wife and I had made an afternoon excursion into the city of St. Louis to eat at one of our favorite restaurants in the area. Since we lived about two hours away, it was a special get away trip from our pastoral responsibilities in Auburn, Illinois. It was a sort of date night into the big city. Our strategy for an early dinner and swift retreat home was being foiled by the early rush-hour work traffic. As I was attempting to make a quick dash to the nearest route toward the Interstate, we drove by

Kiel auditorium, a location of many significant city-wide events. It was quite a sizeable facility, where the building alone covered a whole city block.

There on the huge marquee were the flashing letters announcing the well-known evangelist and healer, Katherine Kuhlman. I had remembered the recent excitement of a pastor friend telling me of her upcoming crusade. I was mildly curious about what took place at her much publicized meetings, but I was also extremely cautious about participating in anything as controversial as a Katherine Kuhlman meeting. I was being drawn without my realizing it, to a place of fuller understanding relating to my own recent experience of being baptized in the Holy Spirit, along with the phenomena known as signs and wonders. I did not however want to give the impression of falling prey to any fringe or fanatical trends.

Beyond my own reluctance, there was also Linda's ongoing apprehension concerning my recent experience of receiving the gift of tongues. I did not want to do anything that would confirm her misgivings that I had betrayed all rationality and had succumbed to some form of alien abduction or extraterrestrial mind control. In addition to her fears, some members of my congregation were becoming alarmed at what they termed radical new changes taking place in worship services, such as alter calls, chorus worship, anointing with oil and praying for the sick. These adjustments represented a departure from the ritual or normal program that made some uncomfortable, even though it was, this religious mindset that I was attempting to change by adding life and spontaneity to the church services.

I had reached that place in my own life where I wanted to know as much of the reality of Christ as possible even experiencing the power of signs and wonders. Linda had remained somewhat skeptical and in a quandary about this whole realm of the present activity of the Holy Spirit. For that reason when Katharine Kuhlman spoke about the Cloud of the Spirit that evening, Linda was determined to check it out. Having directed many large scale dramatic productions in the past, her first thoughts to seeing the Cloud were, "Where's the fog machine? How did they maneuver that cloud into the open area like that?"

It slowly dawned on Linda that she was not seeing something that was imaginary or an illusion brought about by some form of theatrical trickery. Not only did she see the Cloud of the Spirit that day, but she saw what she describes as a mist falling from it. The rain-like substance was falling upon the people as it hung just above their heads. As the mist gently fell, it created physical reactions in the people who were seated under the cloud. While the whole situation seemed beyond the natural realm, Linda was not yet ready to surrender her skeptical position, seeking instead a more rational and natural explanation. All of this was going on while Kuhlman continued to preach.

When Linda first noted the cloud it was exactly where Kuhlman had pointed just minutes earlier in the far left corner of the auditorium. This manifestation of the Spirit began to move toward us on the far right side of the room, as Linda watched it in amazement. Linda became even more attentive to its movement, nudging me to share in her visual astonishment and wonder. Her consternation intensified when I looked to where she was pointing, but saw nothing. As the preacher continued to speak I continued to listen, but Linda was becoming more distraught and distracted by the Cloud. Linda's focus was totally upon that misty phenomena and was giving little or no attention to the message.

Linda continued to interrupt me with her elbow to my ribs, calling my attention to the ominous wonder coming our way. For a time I was able to put off her intrusions, but when she persisted I was forced to speak a quiet word of rebuke concerning her highly unusual and disturbing reactions. My mild scolding went unheeded however, when she abruptly grabbed my arm and warned me that this astounding phenomenon was still approaching us. Her persistence and protest became more verbal as the Cloud was now just a few feet from where we were sitting. I was more than a little surprised, for I had never observed Linda so emotionally over wrought and I certainly had never seen her so disruptive in church. She was so awed by that foreboding and ominous sight that I feared she might be escorted out of the service.

No one else seemed to be alarmed or shocked by anything going on around us. Everybody seemed to be more aware of the true nature of the occurrences than we were. Just a few moments later I turned around to observe Linda sprawled across the theatre seats behind us. She now had my concern and my full attention. We both had a flurry of questions but no answers. Neither of us had a clue of what had just transpired. What could have induced her to cause such a commotion right in the middle of preaching? What was going on? What had just happened? (I had not seen a thing, but I visibly beheld the forceful results for which I had no explanation) From Linda's perspective she wasn't sure whether this aberration was meant for her good or ill. Her situation was made worse by the fact that I was determinedly oblivious to the whole affair.

Linda had seen it all from beginning to end, but had no rationale for what had just taken place. The only thing she knew for sure was that whatever had just taken place was beyond any definition of normal and certainly outside of anything naturally induced. She had been overwhelmed by supernatural power, and knew that she had experienced the awesomeness of a true manifestation of the Holy Spirit and had been dramatically touched by supernatural power. For the first time since her conversion as a child, Linda knew that she had seen and felt the impact of the supernatural Presence of God at work within her own frame of reference. It was all just too real to be ignored or dismissed. That experience of God's visible Presence opened her up to the continued work of the Holy Spirit in her life.

Linda had been raised in a strong evangelical home and had been instructed in many biblical truths, most of which were positive and beneficial because they were foundational and correct beliefs. Linda and I both had been rightly taught that the Bible is the only safe rule for life and practice. Each of us had been taught the importance of being saved and of being a strong witness to others for Christ and the Word of God. We had also been told that miracles and supernatural wonders were not for today. Christ and the apostles performed such signs and wonders only for the purpose of getting the Church established. The gifts of the Spirit were no longer necessary in the church since we now had the Bible. Any time the subject of speaking in tongues arose, it was immediately dismissed as a practice by the fanatical fringe of the Church. We had both been trained in those dispensational doctrines, but the warnings against these matters of the Spirit had been more severe in Linda's family. She had been more sternly exhorted and cautioned about those "unbiblical and over-emotional" people called Pentecostals and especially about their practice of speaking in tongues. Her church even hinted that the use of tongues might even be from the devil. It was also often suggested that Christians should be leery of most emotional displays. Emotionally felt experiences beyond the traditional 'norm' were at least suspect and considered spiritually unhealthy.

As mentioned earlier, I grew up with many of the same teachings as Linda, but since she was raised in a much more active church family she was much more grounded in those beliefs. She was more resistant to the Holy Spirit's manifestation that night because all that she was experiencing went against everything she had been taught; she had been warned against allowing any supernatural experience outside of her original conversion and occasional answers to prayer. Both Linda's parents and church were only feeding her the spiritual diet that had been fed to them by their generational traditions and theological worldview. They were merely handing down and passing on the belief system that they had received. Most of those traditions and doctrines were positive but, like many religious traditions they had become distorted over time by subjective opinions. Their incomplete theology was the result of a background lacking Holy

Spirit experiences creating a lack of openness to new experiences available to them as believers in Christ.

Even though I had not seen what Linda saw or experienced what she had in the Kuhlman miracle service, I still knew without a doubt, that what she was seeing and hearing was from Christ. Neither of us could deny the powerful results of hundreds who were saved and healed that night. I went home that night further convinced of my own experience in being baptized in the Holy Spirit and further determined to live and walk in the Spirit's power. Linda went home that night experientially convinced that Christ was still doing supernatural wonders and that this matter of the Holy Spirit's power was genuine and available to her.

However, God wasn't finished with Linda yet. He had given her one of those indisputable New Testament signs by showing her the Cloud of His glory, but His miracle work in her was just beginning. During the Kuhlman service, evangelist Kuhlman pointed in our direction and made the bold assertion that someone's eyes were being healed. Linda's suspicions were confirmed when she immediately pulled her classes off, but found her seeing was no different. This helped to reinstate or encourage her earlier skepticism. For a few days, Linda thought no more of Kuhlman's prophetic word about eyes being healed. The following week Linda had an eye appointment that had been scheduled several days before the Kuhlman crusade. She had made the appointment for an eye examination for the purpose of getting an updated prescription for new glasses.

After her eye exam, she was informed by the doctor that she, for some reason no longer needed glasses. Shocked by his announcement, she proceeded to argue with the doctor, insisting that she had to have new glasses. She explained to him that she had always worn glasses. She further expressed to the doctor that the last thing she did every night was to pull her glasses off and the first thing she did in the morning was put them back on. She had grown so accustomed to her routine she could hardly consider living any other way. Linda was certain that the doctor had made an obvious mistake. After several minutes of debating with her, the doctor agreed to sell her new glasses with no prescription. Linda came home from the doctor's office that day with glasses having the lowest possible prescription and with 20-20 vision. She had worn glasses for most of her life and her prior prescriptions had all indicated that her vision was getting worse, but God had intervened in her plans of wearing glasses for the rest of her life. She truly had been wonderfully healed unexpectedly by the goodness of God. This blessing had been an unsought and unprecedented miracle touch in her life, but one that thoroughly convinced her of the present-day demonstrations of the Holy Spirit. It would only be a few months after those events that Linda also sought and received the Spirit's empowering Baptism.

My purpose in sharing the above true story is to encourage others of God's supernatural and mighty works today. However, it is also to promote and encourage sensitivity to the Holy Spirit's manifestations in the preaching event. As I observed many years ago in that Kuhlman miracle service, the Holy Spirit may want to manifest His Presence in ways that might be considered beyond the 'normal' service program or preaching agenda. In fact by definition, miraculous wonders are manifestations that operate outside our natural boundaries of comprehension. The fact that God's supernatural wonders are also signs, indicates that they operate with His designed purpose in an attempt to overcome people's natural reluctance to Christ's supernatural manifestations. Experiencing Katherine Kuhlman's ministry of preaching with accompanying signs and wonders was a watershed event for my own growth in appreciating and expecting the miraculous through speaking the Word of God. I am convinced that the force and strength of signs and wonders are the only evidences that have the ability to open us up to the further work of the Spirit. They have the force of touching us at a deeper level and to create in us a greater thirst for more of His presence. Through miraculous wonders a person's awareness can be lifted up or moved past the bondage of tradition and beyond the blindness of an inadequate worldview. Signs and wonders do confirm the words of Jesus when He said, "With God all things are possible" (Mt. 19:26). Signs and wonders may not serve as infallible proofs to everybody, but they do bear a self-affirming and evidential quality to anyone who is honestly seeking Christ.

AN EXPOSITIONAL INQUIRY INTO THE TEXT
Mark 2:1-3; Luke 4:43-44; 5:12-17; Isaiah 6:1-9

It is this author's view that Christians, in general, need to be more aware of Christ's desire to reveal His supernatural signs and wonders as we live and witness throughout our daily lives. It is here assumed that the true Gospel is not just a message to be received intellectually, but is meant to be accompanied by signs and wonders (Mk. 16:20). Unbelievers will be much more enabled to receive the message of Christ when the Gospel is offered not only as a message to be heard with the ear and received as fact, but with a wonder to be seen with the eye as experiential confirmation. Believers are therefore responsible to communicate a Gospel comprised not just of words, but of the works and wonders of the Spirit of Christ.

Those who are called and commissioned to shepherd God's flock are under the same supernatural obligation. We should hold ourselves to the same supernatural standard. It is therefore the premise of this research that supernatural expectation for preaching should be restored to its original apostolic legacy. This is certainly not a new idea, but one that needs to be revived with fresh intentionality and emphasis. That preaching in particular and verbal witnessing in general should be accompanied with supernatural signs and wonders, is as old as the proclamation of Jesus and as new as the Spirit's renewing of the Pentecostal experience in the early twentieth century at Azusa Street.

Even in Pentecostal circles the power of supernatural wonders, in relationship to the actual preaching event, is not a consistent expectation. Almost all Pentecostal preachers I have heard are remarkably good, inspiring and informative, however most have fallen into the classical understanding and traditional practice of viewing the sermon, more as an exercise of listening to homiletic information, than a vehicle for seeing God's miraculous wonders. True to the Scriptures, we anticipate miracles to occur in worship or during Communion and we expect them especially at the time of our altar services. As much as these designated times are commendable, and precious in God's sight, it is this writer's belief that as preachers, we are not taking full advantage of God's most strategic time for miracles. My concern is that even Pentecostals and Charismatics, many of whom have no reservations in believing for miracles and wonders, may slide into, either unintentional lethargy or unconscious bias against them, during the preaching. It is all too easy to lapse into a familiar pattern that views proclamation only as an exercise of the mind for the mind, rather than the opportunity for the Word and Spirit to address the whole person and at every level. Believers in general need to be concerned about this same lack of faith expectancy in verbally witnessing on the streets or in the marketplace. My concern is that the Bible expresses a confidence in the power of the Word of God that the contemporary Church does not emulate.

My focus is not only directed to a heightening of our own expectations as preachers, but through teaching and exhorting our congregations to have a greater anticipation level, when it comes to receiving of God's supernatural visitations. It is the purpose of this writing to stress that our looking for signs and wonders should be at its highest during the proclamation of God's Word under the anointing of the Spirit. This reality should be evident for both the preacher and his believing audience. This sense of expectancy is actually our expression of faith working at several levels. It expresses our faith in the Word of God incarnated, the

Word of God written, the Word of God spoken, and the Word of God still at work in the community of faith, as a *rhema* word today.

I don't sense that God's Spirit-filled people need to be taught these things as much as we need to be reminded of them, that as speakers and listeners we must keep our confidence high acknowledging the genuine power of Christ's proclaimed word. Preachers are known for their many words and the Church is often considered an environment of much speaking. However, the issue is not around the amount of words spoken, but rather do our words have the life and power of the Spirit's anointing? Outreach ministries of the Church are often known for their determination to 'preach' to others but the challenge is to make sure that our witness of the Word is faith filled.

Most of the textbooks on homiletics that I have perused in over fifty years of preaching, have sadly neglected the connection between an atmosphere for miracles and preaching. There may be a few exceptions to this, but I believe this particular focus is unique, in both its distinctive challenge and its singular purpose. I have gained much from all the books on preaching that I have read and surveyed, not only during my years of preaching, but also during my doctoral research on preaching. I have often sat in amazement at the helpful insights and ingenious suggestions that have come from literally hundreds of such volumes. It is therefore with a great sense of humble indebtedness, and yet with a sense of determined conviction, that this volume is dedicated not only to the general witness of the Word but to the specific art and science of preaching. Herein I offer what I believe to be, a needed and even essential component to the privilege and responsibility of the preaching event. The primary intent of this work is not to expand further on the many great books of homiletic theory or technique, but to offer, a workbook which attempts to directly relate the homiletic method to its most original and natural purpose, namely to encourage the mighty works and wonders of God. This text is for the promotion and encouraging of the supernatural results of the Spirit and to enjoy the presence of Christ in all His glory through the power of the spoken Word. It is appropriate to draw our attention to the reality that even our use of terms, like sermon and message, seem to emphasize more the cerebral and cognitive aspects of preaching, than its visceral and experiential purposes.

Since we are speaking of those realities that have to do with the sovereign work of Christ and the will of the Spirit, we acknowledge that no human effort can determine supernatural results. At best, we can only yield ourselves to the work of Christ and the will of the Spirit for their desired ends; but then preaching has always been seen as a task with both a human and divine dimension. The obvious aspect of pulpit oratory is related to the communication skills, personality, character, and passion of the preacher, but these human components of preaching perform a grave disservice to the preaching task, if the whole person of the preacher, and the whole person of the listener are not intentionally recognized. Preaching must be more than one mind addressing other minds. Preaching must come to be viewed as God's special moment and opportunity for Christ's Good News to address and confront persons in their entirety. This idea can also be said to be true for any kind of verbal witness.

In regard to the spiritual, the call to preach has always rested upon a wide range of potentially supernatural expectations. There are several divine dynamics that are associated with the act of preaching such as the nature of the Gospel message itself, the divine character of the preacher's call, the continuity between Old Testament prophesy and New Testament fulfillment in Christ, along with the promise of the Spirit's anticipated anointing. Almost every Christian tradition acknowledges this, so why then should anyone think it strange, that preaching should be recognized as the greatest medium of creating an atmosphere for God's mighty acts and miracles.

In spite of the above spiritual fact, too often Christians seem to feel that it is their moral right and duty, to stand in judgment upon the preached Word. With questions like, "Shouldn't we be discerning about the preaching? Isn't it appropriate to evaluate the sermon? Ought not the believer always to be on guard concerning false doctrines and false spirits?" We offer the answer to all these questions to be an affirming "yes". When believers however, take those questioning prerogatives to an extreme and treat the event of preaching as a merely human act, we are disrespecting both the Word and the Spirit. As Christians, we need to be careful that our response to the preached Word not be the very obstruction that restricts the flow of supernatural supply.

In regard to our faith expectancy, we must remind ourselves that God's supernatural action or revelation cannot be demanded or forced, although we must also remember that miracles most often occur in an environment of faith, confidence, and hope. It is important that our faith and confidence level be at their very highest during the time of preaching, not because of the individual preaching, but because of the essence of the Gospel's power and the Spirit's enabling grace. As the saying goes, it's really not about us, it's all about Him and His ability to make His message come alive, in the reality of the hearer's mind, emotions and body. In allowing God's Word to work, the most significant human ingredient is not so much our skills or even gifts, but our willingness to entrust our meager efforts to His sufficiency, even as we allow our efforts to be interrupted by the will and desire of the Spirit.

Linda and I often reflect back upon that service, where Miss Kuhlman stopped in the middle of her preaching to give the Holy Spirit opportunity to move in an extraordinary and uncommon way. What trust she exhibited in the Spirit's willingness and ability to perform His special works and wonders? When that Cloud of the Spirit appeared and the Lord began to move across that huge auditorium with supernatural effects, Kuhlman's sermon got momentarily overshadowed, at least for those who experienced its effects. She was not intimidated by the Spirit's interruptions she seemed to realize that the Spirit was working even as she continued her preaching. If that had been me, at least at that time in my life, I would have been in total disarray. I would probably have been angry at having to adjust my outline. There is also the inconvenience from such a move and later being able to get back on track of one's theme or topic.

The potential complications of allowing the Spirit's intervention are myriad, and yet, Kuhlman not only allowed the Lord to have His way, but seemed totally unsurprised by what the Lord was doing. She was not irritated by what might be viewed by some of us as an unnecessary interruption or inappropriate disturbance. Many years ago, it began to dawn on me that there was a marked difference between what followed Jesus' preaching and what follows most contemporary preaching, including that of my own. As early as chapter 4 in Matthew's Gospel, we read how closely miracles were connected to Jesus' preaching and teaching (vv. 23-24). It seems clear enough that people responded to Jesus because of both, the revelatory things He said and the miraculous things He did; both connected together were aspects of His ministry. Jesus was ever eager and ready to put His preaching/teaching ministry on temporary hold, in order to perform healing miracles (Matthew 9:18-22; 12:9-13; Mark 1:21-23; 2:2-3; Luke 6: 5-6, 17-18). Jesus' actions to heal were not offered because He thought that preaching was less important, but because the miracles opened more doors to further preaching, they opened up more hearts to receive His preaching, and they were the natural, desired and anticipated result of His preaching.

It is clear that throughout Jesus ministry preaching/teaching and healing/miracles are consistently interconnected. In Mt. 9:35 he acknowledges that in the synagogue, preaching the gospel of the kingdom and healing miracles intersected on a continuous basis. This interweaving of proclamation and power encounters runs throughout the synoptic Gospels. The Gospel of John also reflects an abiding relationship between the works and words of Jesus. For example in 5:36 Jesus says that the very works that He does, bears witness to who He was. Then in 7:46 John records that "No man ever spoke like this Man!" To stress the force and impact of His preaching and teaching, Jesus declares, "The words that I speak to you are spirit, and they are life." (John 6:63). I am convinced that what existed in Jesus' preaching and teaching, should be our intentional goal of proclamation. The speaking of Word and miraculous wonders together represent the interaction and interface, between divine grace and human need.

In Mark 2:1-13, we should be profoundly impacted, not only by the connection between message and miracle, but also with the ease that Jesus continued to minister, given the situation of having the roof over his head ripped off right in the middle of His preaching. While there is much in this passage that is great for preaching with accompanying miracles, my point here relates to the fact that Jesus was unperturbed by the disturbances taking place all around Him. No human action was more important in Jesus' ministry agenda than preaching (Luke 4:43)) and yet His pausing to perform a healing, was completely in character with preaching's purpose.

Even a casual reading of all four Gospels reveals the subtle truth that there was a dialectical pattern to Jesus' ministry. Jesus preached or taught and immediately miracles or mighty works took place. The occurring supernatural wonders drew many others to hear Him speak or to be recipients of His miraculous blessings. This cycle continued throughout Jesus' time upon the earth and He never saw one aspect as competitive to, or interruptive of the other. Even when Jesus exhorted those gathered around Him not to create a crowd-control problem, Luke writes: "However, the report went around concerning Him all the more; and great multitudes came together to hear, and to be healed by Him of their infirmities" (Luke 5: 15). Jesus did not see this as a condition or trait to be criticized or deplored. Rather, He looked upon these despised 'people of the land' with compassion (Luke 7:13; Mark 1:41), and recognized their natural inclination as a supernatural opportunity for Him to glorify the Father (Luke 5:26).

The Isaiah 6:1-8 text is significant because this passage lifts up the biblical expression of God's glory and presence. When Isaiah was in the temple, he had a supernatural vision beholding the glory of heaven, manifested upon that small piece of earthly real estate. It was a revelatory, hallowed and numinous moment when even those heavenly beings came down to participate in the divine experience. It was a Pentecostal moment before Pentecost. The glory of God came down, and Isaiah was cleansed and eagerly took up the prophetic call and anointing. The Old Testament expression of God's Presence was just one of many places, where the Lord's Presence became a manifestation of glory.

The Gospel of John gives a surprising addition to this text when the apostle informs us that it was Christ who confronted Isaiah in the temple (John 12:41). What a profound insight John shares as he adds to our revelatory understanding of Isaiah 6, by giving us the fuller interpretation of the text. It was Jesus whose glory he saw in that worship experience. That glory cloud of the Spirit was the pre-incarnated Son of God who visited with Isaiah, and it was Christ with whom Isaiah had dialogue. What a miracle moment that must have been for the great prophet, to see and hear the very Christ and Lord of the ages, being physically manifested seven hundred years before His birth in Bethlehem. As we preach Jesus today and declare His miraculous manifest glory, we stand in the great lineage of all the ages. We should keep in mind that, when there is genuine revelation coming through the Word, it is Christ's glory and presence still being manifest in His temple of the Church gathered.

Recently Linda and I were having lunch with Pastor Dallas Dean and his wife from Shenandoah, Virginia. He shared with us that one evening he had been invited to speak at a near-by church. He is Pentecostal and the Church that invited him was non-Pentecostal, but appropriate terms of his speaking were agreed upon so he consented to preach. He had barely begun his message, when an unknown lady came running into the Church and begged for assistance. Her son had stopped breathing from a severe asthma attack. She knew her son was in a desperate situation, so she responded with the only option she had and that was to run into the church.

Pastor Dean immediately and without hesitation left the pulpit, ran down the aisle and out the door of the church, to the unresponsive boy in the woman's vehicle. He quickly bent over him and began to pray for life and healing for the lad. Within a short period he was revived and restored to his mother's care. Pastor Dean commented that he had recently run into the mother and the two rejoiced together that after seven years, the young man had never again experienced an asthma attack. But what if Pastor Dean had been more determined to preach his sermon than allow that Word in him to work? This true story stands as yet another example to challenge all preachers to have the sensitivity and confidence to allow the Word they preach to do its work. The authority of the Word and the power of the Spirit truly are sufficient to meet every need.

SUPPORTING QUOTES RELATED TO THE TEXT

"The Spirit is no mere *addendum*. Indeed, he is the *sine qua non*, the essential ingredient, of Christian life. Nor is he a mere datum of theology; rather, he is *experienced* as a powerful presence in their lives. Whatever else may be said of the early church, it was first and foremost comprised of people of the Spirit."[1]

"What we must understand is that the Spirit was the chief element, the primary ingredient, of this new existence. For early believers, it was not merely a matter of getting saved, forgiven, and prepared for heaven. It was above all else to receive the Spirit, to walk into the coming age with power."[2]

"Because for most Christians in the history of the church the Spirit was believed in but scarcely experienced as a powerful presence, either in the individual life or in the community, there grew up the idea that the Spirit was a quite unobtrusive presence. The Spirit was always thought of as a powerful presence. Indeed the terms Spirit and power at times are nearly interchangeable."[3]

"For the earliest believers life in Christ meant life in the Spirit, and that meant life characterized by power, not simply by some quiet, pervasive force. The coming of the Spirit had phenomenological evidence; life was characterized by a dynamic quality, evidenced as often as not by extraordinary phenomena."[4]

"My colleagues in New Testament scholarship may disagree with me here, but I am convinced that the dynamic, empowering dimension of life in the Spirit was the 'norm' in the early church, and that they simply would not have understood the less-than-dynamic quality of life in the Spirit (without the Spirit?) that has been the 'norm' of so much of the later church."[5]

"We have placed emphasis on the sermon and the clergy at the expense of the Spirit. We have prized our versions of decency and order so highly that outpourings of the Spirit pose a threat. Many appear afraid of the Spirit, lest their worlds be shaken and they become swept up into Sabbath play."[6]

"Poor theology can hurt us, for we will miss certain stirrings of the Spirit where we are not expecting them and are not open to them owing to an inadequate doctrinal map. If, on the other hand, places and situations are identified where we ought to be expecting the Spirit to be at work, our eyes may be opened to new possibilities."[7]

"Let us not diminish the importance of the Spirit for Christology. Logos Christology is not the whole story... My point is that Spirit Christology and Logos Christology are complementary, not antithetical...Logos Christology is ontologically focused, while a Spirit Christology is functionally focused, but the two work together."[8]

"As Jesus was empowered, the church is empowered for its mission by the Spirit. Outward forms are not enough—the power must be at work in us (Eph. 3:20; 2 Tim. 3:5). The kingdom of God is not just a matter of talk but of power (1 Cor. 4:20). Outsiders ought to be able to sense the life-changing presence (1 Cor. 14:25). More than churches full of people, God wants (and the world needs) people full of the Spirit."[9]

"Spirit comes in the proclamation of the Word. More than a cognitive issue, this creates a power encounter. Paul says, 'Our message...came to you not in word only, but in power and in the Holy Spirit and with full conviction' (1 Thess. 1:5)."[10]

"As I watched, I saw a church without walls. An awesome divine power was flowing down through the pulpits, out to the people and then through them to the world,"[11]

"By their yielded obedience to the Holy Spirit and His Word they would become reservoirs of truth."[12]

"In preaching actually two are involved, for there must be cooperation between the Spirit of God and the man of God."[13]

"Visualize what you say, and it will vitalize the words as you speak them."[14]

"God was down-to-earth in Jesus Christ. He's up-to-date by the Holy Spirit."[15]

QUESTIONS RELATED TO THE TEXT

1. I have often personally wondered why I never saw the cloud of the Spirit in that Kuhlman service. Intellectually, I can appropriate the fact that it was not visible to me based on what biblical precedent? (Acts 9).

2. Why do we not experience the example of Katharine Kuhlman's preaching as much as we should? To what extent should preachers strive to follow her example?

3. How appropriate was the amount of time that I spent on research and studying the Baptism of the Spirit before receiving it?

4. To what degree should we push others to receive the Baptism of the Spirit? How do you balance the difference between encouraging and pressuring others to receive the Baptism of the Spirit?

5. As believers, to what degree are the gifts and works of the Spirit corrupted by our failure to reflect the character of Christ and the fruits of the Spirit?

6. In all honesty what is your level of expectation of preaching, either as a listener or as a speaker?

7. When we encounter and witness to someone in the workplace or the marketplace how often do we expect or believe for Christ to manifest His kingdom signs and wonders?

CHAPTER SEVEN

ACTS 1:8; 2:17-18; 3:19-21

THE WORD AND THE RESTORING SPIRIT

A NARRATIVE RESPONSE TO THE TEXT

The church choir had finished their special number and was marching single file from the choir loft. As I stood behind the pulpit, Linda stepped from the line and paused beside me just long enough to ask her oft repeated question one final time. In quiet desperation she whispered, "Have you heard anything from the Lord? Do you know what you're going to preach? Has God spoken to you yet?" My own anxiety was apparent when I replied with a simple but frantic "no" to her probes. In eighteen years of preaching, I had never felt more unprepared to preach. In eighteen years of preaching the Gospel, I had never been less prepared to preach. In eighteen years of ministry, I had never gone to the pulpit without a sermon in hand.

It was sermon time and I had nothing to say. I could never have imagined such a predicament of standing behind the pulpit to deliver a sermon that I didn't have. It was like one of those frustrating nightmares where you're scheduled to speak to a crowd and you show up and realize that you've lost your notes. That nightmare was now my reality, except that I was standing before my audience knowing that the message I had prepared I could not preach. I was not sure what I was going to do next nor could I have ever conceived what God was about to do. Based on the prior events of that week, I knew God was up to something for that particular Sunday morning; I simply had no clue or experiential basis for knowing or understanding what was about to take place.

The events leading up to my present dilemma had started on the preceding Monday morning. Mondays were usually a little more relaxing after the pressure of Sunday, and as was my custom I was in my office, browsing through theology books, biblical commentaries and other resources for ideas that might suggest a possible homiletic topic. I would then spend some time flipping through the pages of my Bible for anything that seemed like a germinal seed for a preaching text. Usually by noon on Monday I would have selected my sermon text, located some supporting passages, made a list of several appropriate illustrations and retrieved some personal stories from my memory bank. By the middle of the afternoon I generally had either a written or mental outline of my perspective message. My eagerness to get a quick start on the following Sunday's sermon did not interfere with family life, since Linda was teaching, Angie was in school and Ami was at the baby-sitter's. Having been so regimented and determined, I probably would not have allowed anything to get in the way of my most cherished enterprise of sermon preparation.

Tuesday had become a time of high anticipation since I gave that entire day to writing out my whole sermon in longhand and in manuscript style. I had my text, along with supporting scriptures, my jokes, stories and illustrations carefully prepared and hand written out.

Although I was grudgingly willing to make slight changes if absolutely necessary, it was important to have my homily in its completed form, so that I could start reading through it word for word and line by line. My memory was not all that great so to have the whole sermon memorized by the following Sunday required a speedy finalized version and much effort on my part. It seemed important to me that I have that sermon so well planted in my brain that I could preach it from beginning to end or, if it seemed more appropriate on Sunday morning, I could start in the middle or even turn its main points upside down and preach it. I enjoyed the sense of liberty I felt from not depending on notes and I admit not only a sense of accomplishment but also a feeling of oratory pride. I took joy in stretching myself beyond what I thought I was capable of, but I also thrived on the performance of it all.

Wednesday was my day to become more familiar with my written manuscript by reading it over three or four times. By Wednesday afternoon the sermon was becoming more part of me and my own excitement for the message increased as I gained more of a mental grasp of its content. Up to that point in that week everything seemed quite normal with no surprises. I was feeling an ordinary sense of well-being and calm assurance that all was proceeding on schedule, but that was about to change. Even thought I saw myself as fairly flexible in the face of unexpected interruptions, this particular pattern of sermon preparation had become a good fit with my personality and ministry ego. From this midweek point my anticipation for preaching was already growing. This weekly format also kept me from facing the anxiety of Saturday night crisis preparation and Sunday morning crisis preaching.

Thursday morning my routine had become that of reading through my sermon once, followed by practice preaching with nothing but an outline. This was always a challenge but one that I looked forward to each week. On that particular Thursday I arose and began to follow my homiletic timetable by reading through my message. For some reason my regular procedure didn't fall in line. Not only was my usual plan not working, my thoughts were being interrupted by intrusive along with uninvited ideas. These thoughts were certainly unexpected and unwanted. Right in the midgle of my reading and rehearsing, the words "You can't preach this sermon!" intruded into my mind. This statement was so foreign and unnatural I sought to quickly dismiss it, but the words continued to linger. The impression was not audible to my ears and yet the words were too strong to ignore. At first I gave the statement little credence, but as it was repeated with greater consistency and intensity, I was compelled to consider it. All during that morning every time I started to read or rehearse that message I would receive the same rebuff, "You can't preach this sermon!"

It was all so very irregular not to mention just plain weird. In all my years of preaching this had never happened. I had little doubt as to the source of the voice. I knew I was hearing it inside my head, but I sensed the thoughts were coming from outside my own mind. I was certain that their source was from God. I had been baptized in the Holy Spirit about a year and was beginning to realize that God indeed communicates with us in many and various ways, if we allow ourselves to tune in. I had been growing in my own individual awareness of Christ, through the Holy Spirit's gifts and empowerment, but this occasion had a clarity and certainty to it that surpassed all prior communication. I did not doubt such direct and personal conversation with the Holy Spirit, for Paul says that when we pray in tongues, we are not speaking "unto men, but unto God" (1 Corinthians 14:2). This voice had such force and urgency, that I knew I could not dismiss it.

After determining that the words were from the Lord, my only option was to come into agreement with them. My spirit man said "Okay, if I can't preach this sermon then so be it." However my rational side said, "But why not?" I had no desire or intention of resisting the Spirit, but my first thought was that there must be some doctrinal error in the content, so I read through the whole sermon again just to check for any possible theological or biblical inaccuracies. Even after assessing that the sermon had passed its doctrinal and ethical test, the words again came with the insistence of a command, "You can't preach it!" That was it. I got no further directions, no further information just the negative and insistent command "You can't preach it!" No reasons, no apologies, no regrets, no sympathies and no options were offered. Every quandary as to why I couldn't preach this particular sermon was met by that same relentless and uncompromising "You can't preach it!"

My frustration was becoming apparent. My surface calm and self-assured veneer was cracking under the pressure of not being able to preach a sermon I had worked so diligently on, and where I'd been given no reasons for not preaching it. My reasoning was clear and if there were no apparent theological, biblical or moral reasons for not preaching this particular sermon, then why not preach it? Without being argumentative, I stated my case persuasively, but it seemed that my position did not count. My monologue was going nowhere. I really wasn't trying to be obstinate; on the contrary, I really wanted to be directed by the Holy Spirit and needed to know for sure that this was indeed the Spirit. His statement was so radical that its implications would require my faith and absolute obedience, especially when no explanation was given. Every probe I launched was quickly met with the resolute, "You can't preach it!"

Upon recognizing that this was only a one-way conversation, I changed my tactic from questioning 'why' to 'what'. Since any further insistence on knowing why was an expression of resistance to the will of the Spirit, I simply and politely asked, "If I cannot preach the sermon I prepared, then what do I preach?" That seemed to me like a fair question to ask since Sunday was only three days away. The panic in my voice must have been obvious to the Spirit, for His response was immediate and emphatic. The voice of the Spirit, or at least what I was now sure was the voice of the Holy Spirit, said "Jeremiah!" That was it. That's all that was spoken. Intently I waited for more, but "Jeremiah" was it. I didn't have a clue as to its meaning, but I was sure that's what I heard. I spoke that word "Jeremiah" over to myself several times as I thought about what its significance might be. What was the Lord saying to me? What meaning did that name have in relationship to preparing and preaching on Sunday?

Certainly, I remembered that there was the prophet and book in the Old Testament by that name and I knew that Jeremiah was a present-day common name, but what was the Spirit attempting to communicate with just one word? Did God want me to preach about Jeremiah? If so what did He want me to say about Jeremiah? What could I say about Jeremiah? It was not much to go on. Time was running out and I needed a little more information than just the name of "Jeremiah". Since Jesus while on earth, was best known as a preacher, I knew He understood my dilemma so I made my request known. I wanted help; no I needed help in the worst way; I was really desperate. What should or what could I preach about Jeremiah? Since the idea came from the Lord, surely He had some insights on the topic, so respectfully but boldly I requested several times what it was that I was to say about Jeremiah, but each time all that was echoed back to me was "Jeremiah!" That is all I was getting and apparently that's all I was going to get. I wanted more, but it was clear more was not forthcoming. I felt as if I was on my own without sufficient direction.

I knew that what I heard was from the Lord so I was sure He would guide, but His silence seemed to indicate, or maybe I just I assumed, that the next step was mine. I proceeded to take the most natural course, which was to turn to the biblical book of Jeremiah and begin to read it. Since I had no further clarification, I started with chapter one and began to read as much as I could for the remainder of that day. By the end of Thursday I had completed no more than a fifth of the entire book of Jeremiah. I have never claimed to be a fast reader, but my purpose then was not just to read the book, but more to grasp whatever it was that God thought was important for me to preach on. As I read, I did so in a most prayerful attitude with the full intention of hearing more from the Lord. After every few chapters I consciously paused to request of Him further homiletic information, but after every inquiry the only clear answer I got was the same reply, "Jeremiah!" I wasn't as concerned as I might have been, since I still had Friday to continue my search. The Spirit would surely have mercy regarding my desperate situation; He would most definitely fill in the sermonic gaps tomorrow, I thought.

Thank God, it was Friday! I arose early to continue reading Jeremiah; after all, it's always easier to hear from God in the early morning. I devoted the morning to nothing but reading Jeremiah and listening intently, for anything that might lend itself to a good sermon text from the words of the prophet. I was reminded once again of the many wonderful insights from this great man of God, but nothing seemed to strike a spiritual note relating to a sermon. Again, every few chapters I briefly waited for the Voice to add something, anything would have been encouraging, but nothing was offered; nothing, that is, but that now rather monotonous repetition of "Jeremiah." I continued my relentless pursuit for the rest of that day, with nothing to account for my labor except for an increased familiarity with the book and prophet named Jeremiah.

I had kept my preacher struggles of that week to myself; I had not even told Linda. I guess I didn't want to worry her, but found that it was time for her to join me in my dilemma. I needed someone to share my misery and uneasiness. I knew it would give her cause to be concerned, but I also knew the shock would be worse the longer I waited, so I informed her of all that had transpired those last two days. Sure enough, she was apprehensive about my situation and in fact, I think she was even more worried than I was. She even called some of our closest friends in the church who could grasp the enormity of my plight and began to intercede for me and whatever it was that God wanted to do on Sunday. As the saying goes, "misery loves company" and at least now I was not alone in my bewildering and frustrating journey. I took consolation in the fact that I now had support, and that I still had Saturday left to continue my search for a Sunday sermon.

Saturday morning arrived and I was profoundly hopeful that this would be the day when God would open up the windows of heaven and pour into my heart and mind that long awaited message. I encouraged myself with all the spiritual sounding cliques I could think of, as I continued to read Jeremiah, and bombarded heaven with my urgency for something to preach. With all the spiritual hype I could muster I persevered; my faith was being severely tested. I even found myself at the point of retrieving one of my old sermons on file. I had hundreds and I reasoned, God didn't say I couldn't preach an old sermon; He simply said I couldn't preach the one I had prepared. For a moment I thought I had found a loophole and took satisfaction in my self-deception and mental trickery, but even that didn't last long.

The Holy Spirit was gentle and didn't rebuke my attempt to circumvent His intent. He simply persisted in His unwavering reiteration that the task to keep focused on, that's right, was none other than "Jeremiah." Saturday morning, afternoon and evening passed without any other single bit of information concerning Jeremiah. I would be dishonest if I said that I was not fearful, but my confidence was still holding, for there was still Sunday morning. The service didn't start until 10:30 a.m., therefore I could still finish it before then, if I only had something to finish. That pressurized time frame was not to my liking and would be cutting it shorter than I had ever experienced for preparing a sermon, but it was still doable. While the schedule was not comfortable to my experience or conducive to my pattern, perhaps God was testing my obedience; maybe this was the Spirit's way of stretching my willingness to trust. That was it; that had to be the Spirit's intent; I felt sure of it. I was convinced that the Spirit would pour out the necessary revelatory insights, just in time for me to preach them with great authority and anointing. Sunday morning would be the time of God's great homiletic visitation.

Thank God, as Sunday morning came, I was up to meet the sun and The Son. I couldn't wait to experience whatever great illuminations would come crashing upon my consciousness, so that I could preach like I had never preached before. I was just sure that the message I would be given for that Sunday morning would be as electrifyingly dynamic as was Jonathan Edwards, as he preached that well-known sermon, "Sinners in The Hands of An Angry God." I picked up where I had left off, finishing my reading of Jeremiah. I read and I waited, but there was still nothing. Linda also got up early to hear and listen to whatever great revelations I had received. She was quick to ask, "Have you received anything yet? Has He spoken to you about what you are to preach?" I looked up from my chair and winced as I replied, "Not one word, *nada*, nothing except for "Jeremiah". That's it, that's all I'm getting." Her second question was a very pertinent question to me as well. Anxiously she quizzed, "What are you going to do?" My response was, "I don't know, I guess I'll just open up the book of Jeremiah and start to read." She was trying to be helpful but my words of uncertainty only increased further angst as she blurted out, "Oh no, you can't do that! They won't understand that." I simply shrugged my shoulders and acknowledged, "I know, but that's all I know to do."

With nothing resolved, Linda, the girls and I walked next door to the church. We were nervous and apprehensive, and although I didn't have a plan I was at least hopeful that God had one. I was out on the proverbial homiletic limb. The Lord was going to have to rescue me from that limb, or saw it off. I couldn't ever remember being in such a ministry crisis or preaching predicament, but somehow I knew God was still in control and all I could do was trust. The first part of the service was fairly predictable, although I must say I was hoping for some emergency to take place to extricate me from my anxious circumstances. The hymns and liturgy ended and the choir did their special number and were leaving the choir loft when Linda took advantage of her one last inquiry regarding my desperate plight. That's when she took the opportunity to whisper in my ear that unforgettable query, "Have you heard anything yet? Do you know what you're going to preach? Has God spoken to you yet?" And once more, I spoke my resounding and by this time traumatized, "No!" Again came her frantic probe, "But what are you going to do?" And once more I reiterated, "Jeremiah! That's all I have. That's all I know to do."

After everyone was seated, I paused for just a moment more, to pray for guidance and to give the Lord one final opportunity for

His input; that is, a word other than simply "Jeremiah". Any thing would be of help since I was in no position to bargain or demand. Having still received nothing more, I was committed to proceed with the only thing I did have, and that was the book of Jeremiah. I knew that most would have little appreciation or empathy for my situation, but I had to give some explanation. Therefore I began by briefly acknowledging what had transpired that week. I especially informed them that I had prepared my sermon for that week, but then proceeded to announce to them that God had spoken to me and said that I couldn't preach it, and that all I had been given was the book of Jeremiah. It was obvious by the looks on their faces, and the looks they gave one another, that this was all highly irregular. They had never heard of such a thing as this before from the pastor and they only gave the appearance of cautious acceptance. Their capacity to understand was particularly strained when I commented that God had clearly spoken to me, but since I had always seemed fairly normal in most other respects, they were somewhat tolerant of my explanation.

I then proceeded to open my Bible to the first chapter of Jeremiah and began reading at verse one. "The words of Jeremiah the son of Hilkiah, of the priest that were in Anathoth in the land of Benjamin: To whom the word of the Lord came in the days of Josiah the son of Amon king of Judah, in the thirteenth year of his reign. It came also in the days of Jehoiakim the son Josiah king of Judah, unto the end of the eleventh year of Zedekiah the son of Josiah king of Judah, unto the carrying away of Jerusalem captive in the fifth month" (NIV). Of course, I realized that those verses were just as inspired as any other portion of Holy Scripture and were historically important and textually foundational, but they weren't quite what I needed for a high-powered "stump-jumping" sermon. Linda was right, by the time I reached the end of that passage of scripture, some of the elderly were already nodding off and no one seemed gripped with excitement or visibly enthralled. I continued to publicly read verse 4, "Then the word of the Lord came unto me, saying" (NIV). I recognized that this verse had to be highly significant to Jeremiah, but it wasn't all that dynamically inspiring to me at that moment. So far, nothing was registering on my spiritual radar screen and nothing I had read had noticeably captivated my audience. By this point, I was beginning to feel that this whole scenario was an exercise in futility, not to mention one big, embarrassing fiasco.

If I had been given my preference, I would happily have hidden myself behind the pulpit, or made a quick exit out the side door. In fact, it would have been a great time to have a spring trap door beneath my feet; any method of escape would have been preferable to my uncomfortable and self-conscious situation. Like the Apostle Peter I had stepped out of the boat, the waves were already high and I was sinking fast. The time for emotional protest or spiritual wavering was past; whatever was to happen needed to happen. While noting that all fleshly confidence had dissipated and any hope of extrication unrealized, I decided to continue reading, at least to the end of the first chapter. Suddenly after reading verse four, quite unexpectedly I began to sense a connection, or one might say even a sense of identification, with this prophet of old. I was intrigued enough to continue my public reading of the chapter. As I began to read verse five, something began to stir in me; something beyond my comprehension and totally outside of the dignity of my position as a pastor in one of the great historic denominations. What happened to me, I would not wish upon anyone, especially those considered to be community and religious leaders.

Verse 5 read, "Before I formed thee in the belly I knew thee; and before thou camest forth out of the womb I sanctified thee, and I ordained thee a prophet unto the nations." However, before I read that verse out loud, I read it quickly and quietly to myself. I then started to read it to the congregation, but before I could get out the first four words, "before I formed thee" (NIV). Suddenly and without warning, I broke forth with a gush of tears that could not be restrained. I was caught totally off guard. I was shocked at myself. I was embarrassed. I was bewildered. Here I was standing up in front of 250 people weeping uncontrollably. These were not the actions of a grown man, not to mention that of dignified pastor. This was not the mature demeanor of an educated person. How could this have happened to one who had been trained and disciplined to exegete and explicate a clear and learned discourse? For all my questioning, here I was, barely able to stand, blubbering like a child in public. The whole episode was excruciatingly humiliating.

The more I tried to read, the more I spewed and sputtered. My conclusions ran along these lines: nothing was going as I had assumed, everything was amiss. All was lost! How would I ever live this down? My positional prestige and good name was doomed, I was sure. I had desired to explicate a great revelatory word to the people but what I got, felt and looked, more like a nervous break-down. I could hardly speak, much less preach a stirring and meaningful sermon. Everything was at least very different, even odd. Here I was a thirty-four year old man, at the so called peak of my game, and a fairly sophisticated, intellectual "wannabe." For all my desire to retrieve some measure of professional dignity, I could not stop or even restrain my profuse weeping. This was completely out of character for me, since I could not remember ever shedding a tear in my entire adult life. Linda and I had been married for twelve years and she had never seen me tear up, so you can imagine her surprise to see me so out of control, emotionally. After about fifteen to twenty minutes of this unplanned and unsolicited drama, Linda came up and stood beside me. She explained as much as she could in regard to what was happening, a kindness I greatly appreciated, which offered me a little time to compose myself.

Having regained some measure of emotional decorum, I proceeded to share with the people what had induced such a flood of tears and such an embarrassing eruption. As I began reading that chapter, particularly verses five through ten, the Holy Spirit brought back to my memory a pivotal event I had not thought about for eighteen years. I don't know how I could have forgotten such a crucial moment in my life, since it was foundational to my life's call and ministry. I had not remembered until that moment of reading, that it had been these verses of Scripture that God had used to confirm my call to ministry when I was sixteen years old. How could I have lost the memory of such a pinnacle experience for those eighteen years? That experience had been the bedrock of my life's calling and yet I had buried the very memory of its existence under layers of religious and ministerial activity. Why had I consciously or unconsciously dismissed that watershed moment from my memory banks?

All I could gather was that somehow for almost two decades, I had gotten so wrapped up in doing ministry that I had cut myself off from the very source and stream of my incentive and anointing for ministry. That's what the Holy Spirit had allowed to come rushing back into my conscious awareness after those eighteen years. I had built up such an emotionally protective wall for all those years, that I had continued doing ministry for the most part, in my own strength and training. All that week, without my realizing it, The Spirit had been dismantling that wall piece by piece. Brick by brick, the retaining wall of self-indulgence was being chipped at or weakened until in that single moment, on an unforgettable Sunday morning, the wall crumbled. There I was, standing behind the pulpit, the very image of public ministry, when the dam of imprisoned emotions was broken and my years of inner neglect and lack of Holy Spirit control were washed away. The flood-gates that had remained closed for so long were suddenly opened wide for the work of further spiritual renewal. The Holy Spirit, from that time forward, has had my undivided attention.

AN EXPOSITIONAL INQUIRY INTO THE TEXT
Acts 1:8; 2:17-18; 3:19-21

I was coming to realize also, that the Baptism of the Spirit I had received a year earlier, was not just another spiritual experience but more a renewing epoch of God's ongoing work to restore the spiritual man that had gotten lost along the way. The longer I live and minister, the more I become aware that the great work of the Holy Spirit is continuing with the restoring of the whole person. I am convinced that in the last days, the Lord has one final component that He desires to restore to the Church in general and to ministers in particular, and that is His restoration of witness and preaching that produces signs and wonders to confirm it.

I chose the three passages from the Book of Acts that opens this chapter to emphasize the historic flow of Christ's intent and strategy for the Holy Spirit in the lives of all believers. Acts 1:8 recalls Christ's initial **promise** of the Spirit to the disciples, who represented both the structural foundation and the experiential pattern for the Church. This single verse also indicates the missional model that the Church must follow throughout its history, if it is to stay in step, and stay on course, with the risen Lord. The first step of this ecclesiastical pattern promised the disciples that they were going to receive an unprecedented, unexpected power dynamic we have come to call Baptism in the Holy Spirit. This new impartation would change them in order to change the world.

This power would bring new enablement to witness, that would also result in a new expression of worship and a heightened faith, thereby ushering in an astonishing, fresh wave of kingdom wonders. Jesus knew that, with all the disappointment the disciples had faced and the trauma of rejection yet to come, the most important addition they would need was power. If they were to consider making an impact upon their unbelieving surroundings and fulfilling Jesus' mandate, they would need His enablement power. In explanation of this verse, F. F. Bruce comments: "Instead of the political power which had once been the object of their ambitions, a power far greater and nobler would be theirs. When the Holy Spirit came upon them, Jesus assured them, they would be vested with heavenly power—that power by which, in the event, their mighty works were accomplished and their preaching made effective."[1]

It should be further noted that their newly appropriated abilities from heaven were meant to be used for transacting the business of earth in accordance with the supernatural methods of heaven. The natural gifts of rhetoric and oratory would not suffice to convince the same crowd that had just a short time before demanded blood. After killing Christ their leader, the disciples understood well enough that their neighbors and fellow Jews wouldn't think twice about murdering them also, all in the name of the Law. This hostile environment, along with the physical ascension of Jesus which left them to fend for themselves, was enough to strike fear in their hearts. There was no doubt about it, they would need an awesome power to strengthen themselves and one another, for every aspect of their existence.

It must always be kept in mind that this power, spoken of by Luke, is not just any power for any purpose. It was not power for power's sake. It was not power for personal prowess or power for self display. It was a power of supernatural design for a missionary purpose. It was a power for witness to grasp the full understanding of what Christ had accomplished on the Cross and by His Resurrection; all of His authority and power for ministry was now available to His followers. The benefits and blessings that abundantly poured forth from the gracious heart of Christ, could now flow from the lips and hands of every believer.

The promise of this power was to make Christ known in ever widening circles from "Jerusalem and in all Judea and Samaria, and to the ends of the earth" (Acts 1:8). This pronouncement would serve as the divine declaration of how the Church was to proceed. It was a direct order from the Commander-in-Chief, and not to be disregarded. It would be the divine program and plan for worldwide expansion. Christ's announced strategy in this verse suggests the ever extending circles, not only for the collective mission of the Church, but also in regard to the expected and inward compulsion of every believer after the Holy Spirit came upon them. Again, in the words of Bruce, "In Acts we do not find an apostolic succession in the ecclesiastical sense, nor a succession of orthodox tradition, but a succession of witness to Christ."[2] The geographical areas noted here reflect not only the theme of the whole book of Acts, but the global challenge and agenda of the Gospel for the entire Church age. It represents the never ending spiral of witness in the dynamic of the Spirit until the kingdom now becomes the kingdom of the future.

The second passage listed is found in Acts 2:17-19. These verses are an Old Testament reminder of the kind of **power** that Spirit-enabled believers should anticipate and demonstrate. The prophet Joel refers to "the last days" or "the age to come" (2:17) and fit exactly with what Luke wants to expand upon, meaning that "the sign of the age to come is the presence of the Spirit,"[3] to again use the words of Bruce. The prophet Joel is predicting that when the Spirit is poured out "on all flesh," the entire cosmos would be charged with supernatural energy and illuminating light. The effects of this new source of spiritual energy would be seen and heard in both heaven and earth, among old and young, male and female, Israelite and Gentile, pampered and pauper, in their present time and for every other unfolding future age.

Concerning the above passage George Woods writes, "God promised not to favor the early over the late. He blesses both the first to hear and the last...Acts 2:39 says there is no time limit on receiving the gift of the Holy Spirit. This gift is for their parents, their children, and those of every generation and race."[4] To realize the eternal truth of this statement, one has only to seek and ask. This Baptism in the Holy Spirit, with its resulting miraculous manifestations, is the greatest of all the expressions of God's unmerited grace towards His children. It is just as Woods further exclaims, "Wow! What good news this is to all. God is not biased. He has no favorites. He will pour out His Holy Spirit on all. Pentecost is for everyone. Those of any race, gender, age, and social level, may drink of His Spirit at any time. Whosoever will, may come."[5]

The third passage to be considered is that of Acts 3:19-21. This text focuses on Christ's completing the intentional work of the Spirit for the **purpose** of undoing the works of the devil. Christ's full purpose for mankind can be seen in these verses, for they speak of repentance, refreshing and restoration. Of course Christ's work of regeneration is necessary for our spiritual pardon and His sanctifying grace is essential for our moral purity, but His equipping is also mandatory for our operating from our authoritative position. Our pardon, purity and position in Christ are all important to complete the total ministry of Christ for, in and through us. It takes all three aspects of Christ's redemptive work to fulfill His desired destiny toward us, in us, for us, then through us.

The results of our pardon, purity and position in Christ corresponds to the three categories in verses 19-21 that addresses the ministry of the Spirit that calls us to repent, to enjoy times of refreshing and to anticipate the effects of full restoration. These are all connected and intertwined, although they are also different aspects of Christ's work through the Spirit. Repentance is foundational, not only for entrance into the dimension of Christ's kingdom, but also as the required attitude for developing in the life of His kingdom. Refreshing is the intended benefit of the Spirit as we are faithful in worship, work and witness. The "times of refreshing" referred to here, are reflective of Christ's ongoing renewing process as we live by the Spirit.

Restoration is representative of the Spirit's determination to recreate in us and reclaim for us, all that Satan has taken from us. Jesus described the devil most precisely when He called him "the thief" (John 10:10), and warned us that he "does not come except to steal, and to kill, and to destroy" (John 10:10). Jesus' birth, life death, resurrection, ascension and Spirit outpouring was directed to the work of complete restoration through changed lives, defeat of dark forces, demonstrations of signs and wonders and final renovation of the earth at His return. Restoration is Christ's work in three tenses. In Christ we were positionally restored (Eph. 2:6) at conversion, we are being restored as we allow the Spirit to operate in us (fruits of the Spirit as listed in Gal. 5:22-23) and through us (gifts of the Spirit as given in I Co. 12:8-10) and we will be completely restored either at the Rapture of the saints or the Resurrection of the dead.

It was the present tense of Christ's restorative ministry that was being activated in my story about the Spirit's intervention on that day I tried to preach, but could only weep. Of course it is that same tense that will continue to work in my life and ministry until He comes or at my death. I am still awaiting an even greater expression of His work of restoration, in relationship to a preaching ministry that will be characterized by an unprecedented anointing for signs and wonders. This preacher is believing and living in expectation of a time when his preaching will result in a shock wave of supernatural miracles every time he is honored to stand behind the pulpit or even in the market place.

I believe that we have too long allowed the enemy to rob from the Church and the proclamation event, its original power and purpose for ushering in the glorious presence of God with its accompanying supernatural demonstrations. My greatest longing and confident expectation is that this kind of witness will characterize my ministry and that of the end time Church. My deep desire is to help train a cadre of young men and women to rise up to this challenging expectation and to even move beyond this present generation in Holy Spirit empowered preaching. I pray that my forty years as a pastor and eight years of being connected to the Bahamas as academic dean and teacher throughout those islands, will result in a greater impact of the miraculous through every form of verbal witness. It is my desire that the students I have taught in several countries have been impacted to expect their preaching to be confirmed by signs and wonders. As present director and professor of the Missions Department at Zion Bible College (soon to be Northpoint Bible College), it is my hope that all our students will be inspired to go into the whole world and preach the Gospel with signs following.

The biblical cycle here in Acts chapter three, is typical of the ongoing links between miracle and preaching. In verses 1-11, Luke relates the magnificent healing of the lame man at the Temple's gate "called Beautiful" (v. 2). This miracle provided Peter another opportunity to preach (v. 12). In Chapter four of Acts, the wide-spread report of the healing gave yet another chance for witness and we begin to see the familiar pattern found in the Book of Acts. Dr. George Woods affirms that "here, as in Acts 2:14-36, we see an emerging pattern for preaching of the gospel."[6] In concluding this exegetical and expositional section, I wish to simply note that, just as in the book of Acts believers would come to know Christ more deeply by the Baptism of the Holy Spirit and fire (Mt 3:11), I too would come to know Him, but then that's another story.

SUPPORTING QUOTES RELATED TO THE TEXT

"Luke's perspective on 'signs and wonders' is rich and full. He clearly acknowledges the important role that miracles played in the ministries of Jesus and the early church. His narrative is replete with references to the miraculous. At almost every opportunity, he reminds us that word and sign go hand and hand."[7]

"Luke's attitude toward 'signs and wonders' may be described as positive, but not uncritical. This is most clearly reflected in his emphasis on proclamation. For Luke, the primary manifestation of the Spirit is not miracle-working power, but rather bold and inspired witness."[8]

"The last 2,000 years of history show us that a revival will come and last two to four years, then fade out. Because of this pattern, an entire branch of theology has developed that says revival is supposed to arrive periodically to give the

Church a shot in the arm—new enthusiasm, new hunger, new energy. But by saying that revival is an exception, a pit stop for refueling, normal Christianity is defined way down. I say rather that revival is not the exception; revival is normal. Signs, wonders, and miracles are as normal to the gospel as it is normal for you to get up in the morning and breathe."[9]

"God showed me that my capacities and my theological training were insufficient. The world does not need theology. The world needs *life*. From that moment I experienced a thirst and hunger for spiritual power, a longing to know the Holy Spirit. I needed an anointing to break hardened hearts, an anointing that shatters the devil's chains and makes the light of Christ shine."[10]

"The Bible is filled with all sorts of promises…Fantastic promises all, but none is more fantastic than this: 'I tell you the truth, anyone who has faith in me will do what I have been doing. He will do even greater things than these, because I am going to the Father' (John 14:12). If this even comes close to the truth, then mustn't we confess we have never taken Jesus seriously? The least we have to confess is that we have been satisfied with far less than he promised and far less than is possible."[11]

"That is the redemptive purpose of the gifts. It's not just bringing people to salvation, but also restoring them to the purpose of God for their lives…Redemption involves restoration and reconciliation. The Holy Spirit uses the manifestations of His gifts to restore broken relationships and to bring people back to intimacy with the Father, and such is the purpose and function of all the gifts of the Spirit."[12]

QUESTIONS RELATED TO THE TEXT

1. Some writers choose to view the work of restoration as synonymous with redemption rather than the important completing work of redemption. What are some scriptures that might support either view?

2. Why must the work of redemption precede all other work of restoration, reconciliation or sanctification?

3. Is it fair to say that redemption is more of an immediate act in us, whereas restoration is more of an ongoing process upon us? Why or why not?

4. How has the ministry of the Spirit worked in your life in relation to repentance, refreshing and restoration?

5. In what way does our positional authority in Christ affect our witness and in what ways should it affect our confidence in preaching results?

6. How does Pentecost, as the sign of the age of the Spirit, impinge upon both our view of miracles and our expectancy of the preaching event?

7. Do you see a consistent cycle or a continuing dialectical pattern between Jesus' preaching and miraculous wonders?

8. How and in what situations is it possible to glorify miracle over message?

9. From your perspective should Bible believers really see revival as the accepted rule for the Church or as temporary exceptions?

10. How should preaching as seen in the New Testament both encourage us and at the same time challenge us?

CHAPTER EIGHT

MATTHEW 3:11; ACTS 2:3; LUKE 12:49; I KINGS 18:24

PREACHING: SPEAKING THE WORD; SPREADING THE FIRE

A NARRATIVE RESPONSE TO THE TEXT

Our Sunday night service was just concluding when one of the ushers came to get me and Linda and took us to the back of the church. There stood five young boys and girls, which we quickly recognized as children from the neighborhood. As Linda and I approached them we could see the quandary on all their faces and sensed the emotion that registered in their voices and actions. The children had, just moments before, come rushing through the doors of the church into the foyer where the ushers had first encountered them and asked them what they wanted. The children were speaking with such excitement and speed that they were difficult to understand, but their faces reflected a sight so remarkable that it had to be shared.

One by one each child managed to explain the source of both their enthusiasm and concern. With eyes as big as they could be and stammering lips they were unanimously expressing their wonder, "we wanted to come and ask if we should call the fire trucks because we're seeing fire on the roof of the church!" Although it was an old building and nobody knew how bad the wiring may have been, there was no sign of the fire, yet these children were so sure that they had just seen, only moments before, genuine fire on the roof. For a time none of us were sure what to make of it all, but it prompted a lot of discussion at the time and for me, the event encouraged a research into the biblical revealing of the Holy Spirit and fire. Since that event, now many years ago, I have read and discussed the connection of fire as a manifestation of spiritual revival throughout Church History. That evening's experience with the children, and along with vast reading about revival movements, has convinced me that what those neighborhood children saw that night was indeed a manifestation of the Spirit's presence and power. For that reason the theme of our ministry for many years now has been "spreading the fire of the Spirit." Whether I have been a pastor of a church, teacher at a Bible college or serving as a missionary educator "spreading the fire" has been my message; for approximately thirty-nine years, and counting that has been my ministry focus and the content of my message. It is my deep conviction that without the Spirit's fire (Mt. 3:11), we can not fully and adequately present the message of Christ. Pentecost is the source of the believer's empowerment and enablement but, before I go any further allow me to share the reason that the Spirit revealed Himself in such a visible and extraordinary way at that Sunday night service.

Those Sunday night services had been started to provide a place for those newly baptized in the Holy Spirit to worship in the freedom of the Spirit, in a less structured atmosphere than the traditional service. These evening services were also offered to extend an open opportunity for church members to experience a personal conversion and receive the fullness of the Spirit and had been established as an environment invitational to people seeking healing in their bodies and their relationships. However, what was about to happen was neither scheduled, planned or even anticipated.

There had been both powerful worship and preaching by the guest evangelist including a call to the altar for salvation and for the Baptism in the Holy Spirit. Although my wife and I had come to hope for and expect miracles and wonders, we were not prepared for what took place on that occasion. Fortunately, we had a guest minister that night who was more experienced than we, in certain spiritual realities and biblical practices. During the altar call a young couple came up who I had recently prayed with to receive Christ as personal Savior. Both had now come to the altar to ask for prayer to receive the Baptism in the Holy Spirit with the sign evidence of speaking in tongues.

Being confident of their salvation, my wife and I along with the evangelist laid hands on them and began to pray. Bob received both quickly and powerfully, but as we continued to pray, Lori slid to the floor. At first, we all thought that she had simply become overwhelmed by the Holy Spirit (called slain in the Spirit) so we continued to pray. Although, all of us soon began to realize that there was something spiritual at work within her, but it certainly wasn't the Holy Spirit. The evangelist's own experience and our corporate discernment brought us painful awareness that what we were dealing with was not the Holy Spirit's touch on her.

Lori began to act in a way that was beyond anything I had ever witnessed. After she dropped to the floor, she curled up into a fetal position and made no movement or sound. For quite some time she simply lay there in a motionless state. I still did not have full understanding as to what was going on, but the whole scene was just too odd to ignore. I could sense that Lori's actions were out of context to my knowledge of her and that there was something sinister about the situation; all of us were uncertain about what to do next. Soon it became clear that we were dealing with demonic oppression. I knew that according to Scripture, demons had to be verbally cast out and could not simply be prayed away. We continued to cover the situation in prayer, but now also began to command the demons to release her.

We were doing all we knew to do, but nothing observable was noted in Lori. No one on the ministering team felt as if we had enough information to go further. Therefore, we continued to ask

Bob to probe his memory concerning anything that could have triggered this reaction in Lori; it had only been her requesting prayer for the Baptism in the Holy Spirit that seemed to precipitate this whole situation. Every time we encouraged Bob to reflect upon any occult involvement or demonic invitation his wife may have encountered in the past, Lori, without a sound being uttered or demonstrating any previous movement, slide her hand toward Bob and yanked at his pant leg. This was noted as having happened several times, even as she otherwise remained in her motionless, trance-like position. The result would always be the same; each time Bob would start to say something, Lori would give a tug and Bob would immediately cease whatever he was about to speak. We were beginning to realize that Bob, Lori and this spirit presence knew something we needed to know also.

We questioned Bob about any unusual situations that Lori had confronted recently. We continued to inquire if he knew of any circumstances that possibly could have caused her to react in this way. Anything might help us know more about what we were facing and dealing with. He thought for a moment, but replied that he knew of nothing irregular that might cause her to respond in this unexpected manner. We continued our ministry to her with nothing to go on, except that every time we talked to Bob and every time he started to say anything, her arm would slither across the floor, grab a hold of his leg and shake his pant leg fiercely. We did not want to be rude or pushy with Bob, but it was apparent that he was privy to some information that would help us free Lori from her spiritual bondage. This strange behavior seemed to confirm that we were dealing with a definite demonic spirit.

Finally despite Lori's ongoing disruptive maneuvering, Bob began to recount to us something that had happened to her in the past. While unsure that it had any relevance, he began to tell us about an occurrence that had taken place in Lori's life four or five years earlier, while she was a student at one of our state universities. Lori had been driving down the highway when she passed a woman who seemed to know her resulting in their each pulling off to the side of the road. Although they had never met, the lady began to tell Lori things about herself that a stranger would never have known. Gaining Lori's full attention she then began to give Lori an astrological reading of her life, informing Lori that she would be in an automobile accident that would be connected to water. She also warned Lori that if she tried to rescue the other person in her car, both would drown but if she chose to do so she would be able to swim to safety alone. Having predicted this to Lori, the lady then got into her car and drove off.

For several years Lori had lived with griping fear and terror, being constantly reminded of her foretold and foreboding future. Every time she got into a vehicle, that foreboding prediction remained as a dark and destined potential reality in her mind. For all those years Lori had lived with the fear and anxiety of wondering when her foretold accident would occur. She often worried about the decision she would be forced to make, regarding the passenger in her car when the accident took place. Lori's anxiety concerning her predicted event laid heavily on her mind like an unchangeable and inevitable reality and actually created in her an atmosphere of dread. It was always with her, so much so in fact that during that period she had several automobile accidents. It hung over her head as a self fulfilling prophesy that she would one day inextricably experience. The enemy's tool of lies and deceptions had accomplished their purpose in those several years between that college encounter and that Sunday evening service.

My assessment of the present situation was that the spirit wanted to keep Lori in the grip of its dark clutches, by hiding within a cloak of anonymity, but possibly without realizing it, Bob had divulged to us the source of the devil's hold on Lori. The ministry team recognized that the demonic chain that kept Lori imprisoned for several years had been forged by links called fear, anxiety, dread and self-incrimination. All those emotional responses began on that day when a self-proclaimed witch spoke her destructive spell on Lori. Lori became powerless over time to break the self-destructive behavior pattern that had been established until that time when the whole deliverance team began to bind the spirit of witchcraft that had been oppressing her. It only took a few minutes of this kind of spiritual warfare and authoritative command to allow Lori to be totally set free of that harassing presence. She could then quickly and beautifully stand, beginning to pray and worship the Lord her Rescuer in a new tongue of spiritual liberation and joyous freedom.

While there is much more to the story of that particular deliverance, especially as it pertained to what was going on in Lori's own thoughts and emotions, to her certain deliverance from that tormenting spirit there can be no doubt. To reference further the devil's desire to destroy Lori, one has only to remember the many accidents Lori experienced because of that fear which had been implanted by the spirit of witchcraft. In fact, she had been so severally injured in one of those many accidents that doctors had told her that she would never be able to bear children. However, as Bob and Lori committed themselves to honor the Lord, the Lord healed Lori of that diagnosis. How can one be so sure of His divine intervention? Bob and Lori went on in the Lord to experience the birth of five beautiful children.

That experience taught me something about the devil's attributes that can be stated as follows: *Since Satan doesn't know the future, he tries to create it through the evil seeds of deception and dread implanted by any means possible.* I believe that this is the particular strategy that Satan uses, when it comes to both cultic and occult activities. As Bob and Lori's story shows, the devil is a liar, but being neither omniscient nor omnipotent, he attempts to force a person's destiny through subterfuge and manipulation. Since he does not have power over one's future, his ploy is to get people to believe his trickery and to choose their own destruction, through allurements into forbidden contacts and connections with the spirit world where he can influence them.

Most importantly, however, is what I learned about the goodness and greatness of God through that deliverance confrontation. I acquired an indelible confidence that, through faith in Christ, every scheme of the devil can be reversed. According to Satan's plans, Lori was programmed to live under the tyranny of fear and caught within an ever circling routine of accidents that would ultimately lead to another's death and perhaps her own. Through her faith in Christ, the enemy of her soul no longer had the last word; through her desire for all that Christ had provided to her she was able to step into the freedom that God had already designed for her. Through faith in His all encompassing provision, Bob and Lori were able to fulfill their purpose both in Christ's Kingdom, the church and in their family. Although, Bob and Lori were not immune to tragedy without His delivering power and healing grace, Bob and Lori would not have even had a family.

The truth gained during that evening's deliverance would be confirmed through many other demonic encounters, where Linda and I would see persons and families set free by the power of the Holy Spirit's fire and presence. I believe that it is the fiery presence of the Holy Spirit that is required for people to be set free from Satan's grasp. I believe that it is only the presence of the Holy Spirit and fire operating in the Body of Christ that can turn believers into firebrands for the Kingdom of God. Only as the Church takes hold of the Pentecostal message of the Holy Spirit and fire will the world be confronted with the life-changing experience of the Kingdom. Only the Holy Spirit and fire can ignite our passion to see people set free and to force the enemy of man's soul to return and restore all he has stolen from them and the Church. It is my contention that one of the most important ministries to be restored to the present-day Church is Christ's work of deliverance. When this ministry is neglected by the Church, those spirits of darkness or evil may even find the Church a sanctuary to be as safe a place to hide in as any. We must determine that dark spirits not feel as comfortable in the Church in our day as they did in the synagogue of Jesus' day.

Deliverance ministry is, I believe, the work of every Spirit-filled believer and not only for a select few. It is also important that the work of deliverance be done alongside all the liberating and healing ministries of the Church. However, for believers to function in this labor of love extended to the oppressed, they require the enablement of "the Holy Spirit and fire" (Mt. 3:11), for nothing less will accomplish the task. It will be those who are willing to step on to the field of battle who will discover the overwhelming sufficiency of "the Holy Spirit and fire" (Lk. 3:16). I have been blessed to be able to preach and teach throughout the U. S. as well as in South America, Canada, Africa, Hong Kong, Taiwan, China and the Caribbean Islands. I can state with all assurance that, only as we proclaim the Gospel of the Kingdom with the "Holy Spirit and fire" can anything of significance be accomplished to expand or extend that Kingdom. The Body of Christ must continue to ring out the Evangelical requirement for individual salvation, the Liberal call for unity in Christ, the Charismatic insistence on growth in the Spirit's gifts, the Wesleyan encouragement toward holiness, the Third Wave's challenge to minister through signs and wonders and the Pentecostal mandate to experience "the Baptism in the Holy Spirit and fire" (Mt. 3:11).

AN EXPOSITIONAL INQUIRY INTO THE TEXT
Matthew 3:11; Acts 2:3; Luke 12:49; 1 Kings 18:24

Only the message of the Gospel expounded with the anointing of the Holy Spirit and fire can give to the Church a fresh awakening of God's end-time purposes. It is this preacher's assessment that the world deserves to witness this kind of Church today. It is my contention that the world will not even hear the Gospel until they also see it manifested in all of its glory and power, which is only by the anointing of "the Holy Spirit and fire". Truly the Gospel of Christ is not a tame message allowing us to continue on our merry way unchallenged, it is the Word of God that breaks through all of our rationalistic facades with a compunction and compassion that longs to see people truly set free from all demons, whether they be demons of animism, rationalism or traditionalism.

America is being overrun with all kinds of demonic forces. We have been invaded by every form of demon from cult religions to occult practices such as witchcraft. Yet our worst demons are those that are more polite, more subtle. They are the demons that attract believers into a materialistic version of Christianity, whose only desire is for material prosperity, or into a cultural form of westernized Christianity that embraces "a form of godliness but denying its power." (2 Tim. 3:5). It is a gospel with a split personality. Much of the American Church preaches a gospel that has its origins in the historic Gospel of Christ, but has settled for a gospel that is more akin to Greek enlightenment, than biblical revelation. The emphasis is more on the brilliance of the human mind, exact sermonic structure and precision of human language than on the grace that flows from the Spirit or the impact of the anointed Word.

Much of the gospel that is preached from our church pulpits resembles more the form of Greek oratory than the preached Word of Jesus and the apostles. When Jesus preached, the fire of the Spirit saved lives, healed and resurrected bodies and cast out demons with the power of a Word. When the early believers went out to spread Christ's Gospel they also had the same force and energy to deliver people from all the wiles of the devil. Some present day leaders are so bound by tradition that they will admit that a Gospel of power is needed for the primitive tribesman, or for the less educated cultures of our globe, but think that only a rational Gospel will work for our more westernized society with its more cultured sensibilities. However, it is my deep conviction that those who have embraced a more naturalistic paradigm or humanistic philosophy are in just as desperate a need for a Gospel of power as the African witchdoctor. Who knows, but that persons bound by enlightened rationalism are not in the greater need for the miraculous works of the Holy Spirit and fire! It has been well documented that the spirits of western religion and traditions can be the most resistant to the real truth of the Gospel. If truth remains only in the realm of the intellect, it negates both the revelational content and the power of the Gospel. But, by the ongoing and constant experiences of the Holy Spirit the Gospel becomes increasingly relevant and vibrant.

The first Scripture text to examine in this chapter is from Matthew 3:11. I selected this text because, after years of reading that verse I must admit that I was clueless as to its intended significance. Having been evangelical for years I accepted the statement that John spoke in regards to Jesus, when he said "I indeed baptize you with water unto repentance, but He who is coming after…will baptize you in the Holy Spirit and fire." I accepted it because it was Scripture, but understood the phrase "the Holy Spirit and fire" to mean a symbolic referencing the necessary work of the Spirit both in the Old and New Testaments. I also had come to believe that when I accepted Christ I had already received all of the Holy Spirit and fire that anyone had a right to expect, therefore I rested in the confidence that I had already experienced this fullness of the Holy Spirit and fire, thereby walling myself off from any further interaction with His flaming presence. I was satisfied and complete in both my teaching and my experience.

By the time I finished my Masters of Divinity degree from a theologically liberal seminary, I learned that not much of what I had been taught or had experienced mattered much. I had learned that any experience of God was at the very least inconsequential and at the very most a hindrance, especially to my intellectual and psychological development. I acquired the more sophisticated position that phrases like "the Holy Spirit and fire" were nothing more than cultural aphorisms, primitive legends or Jewish idioms. True scholarship implied the attitude of negative critique toward anything related to true revelation or genuine miracle.

I still have an appreciation for the research and study tools that seminary training introduced me to, but it did much to diminish the sense of Christ's continuing and empowering work through the Spirit. It was the experience of the Baptism in the Holy Spirit that began an awareness of a greater love and appreciation of what it is that Christ has truly provided for us. I also became more aware of a new understanding of the uniqueness and wonder of the written Word. I began to allow the Bible to speak for itself and embraced a growing hunger to receive the insights that the Spirit alone could give. Gradually, sermon preparation took on an ever deepening dynamic for me. Since the revelation of the Word is boundless and the wisdom of the Spirit is without limits, there should never be a point of arrival but always an ongoing process of arriving. My personal journey in preaching is ever about having a hermeneutic that is developing around the innate profundity of the Word and the consistent counsel of the Spirit to make it practically simple and powerfully relevant.

Without meaning to disparage my academic training, I came to realize that after having been baptized in the Holy Spirit, I had come to know more about Jesus and the Bible in one year than I had acquired in eight years of academia. While there will always be an importance connected to a foundation in academic scholarship, it must never be allowed to substitute for what the Holy Spirit can and will reveal to us, about the goodness and the greatness of Christ. It is my conclusion that when it comes to matters of spiritual reality, we often rely too heavily on the knowledge of 'experts' and far to little on common sense, spiritual experience and a devotional appropriation of the Word. By all means read the biblical commentaries, the Bible dictionaries and study the concordances, for they have many good insights and great informational content to offer, but do not allow them to rob the preaching event of its supernatural capacity to unveil new heights of wonder and glory.

Yes, "the Holy Spirit and fire" can still drive out before it all the "serpents and scorpions" (Luke 10: 19) that the devil provides to cause hurt and pain to all mankind. William Barclay describes the fire's abilities well: "The desert had in places thin, short, dried-up grass, and stunted thorn bushes, brittle for want of moisture. Sometimes a desert fire would break out. When that happened, the fire swept like a river of flame across the grass and the bushes, for they were as dry as tinder. And in front of the fire there would come scurrying and hurrying the snakes, the scorpions…They were driven from their lairs by this river of flame, and they ran for their lives before it."[1]

Certainly the above bit of knowledge is encouraging and should always be appreciated. Also, acknowledging that Jesus demonstrated the reality of this truth through His own ministry explaining and teaching it to His disciples provides the evidence of a connection between preaching and miracle. However, what of persons today who suffer under the constant barrage of Satan's attacks? What about a person in this generation who believes he or she must endure the brokenness of their spirit's imprisonment, bodily afflictions, with mental and emotional torment and lives ruined by the dark forces that hide in the underbrush of secret and shameful deeds? Many, even most of these desire to be set free, but are bound by the lie that the chains holding them are too strong to be torn away.

Pardon me for sounding so affirmative, but our solution is so simply biblical. The Church's hope still lies in the simple message of Pentecost found in Acts 2 where the supernatural manifestation of fire prompted the even greater demonstration of Spirit-empowered preaching which in turn initiated the greatest spiritual awakening of all time. The Book of Acts is an account of miraculous wonders because the flaming message that instigated this new era of Christ's eschatological kingdom is found in the dynamic of the Holy Spirit.

It was the preached Word by Peter, one of God's least educated and most compulsive servants that launched the present age of the Spirit and equipped the Church for her task. It was the early believers' witness that birthed the beginning of God's new day, when believers in Christ would start to reclaim the spiritual legacy that belongs to God's redeemed people. While it is true that we don't require another historical Pentecost, we certainly must have a new igniting of "the Holy Spirit and fire" to overcome our present spiritual and moral lethargy through proclamation of the Word with signs following. Just as the fire of the Pentecostal message spread to the entire world from the Azusa Street revival, so we are in need of a rekindling of that same fiery glow in our preaching.

The Holy Spirit, allowed to work again in the life of the Church with the compassionate power of deliverance, will obliterate the restricting powers of the devil's domain. Only by the Spirit's renewal can we freely invade the devil's once forbidden territory and demand in Jesus ' Name what he has wrongfully taken hostage. We have the authority to set fires of revival to expose his hiding places and to drive him from human habitations where he has taken up residence in the souls of men and women, boys and girls. I even believe that the proclaimed Gospel is the best method of bringing deliverance from demonic oppression whether from the pulpit or in the market place. We rightly think of the spoken word as speaking to people, but I believe that we need to be sensitive to "the Spirit and fire" in order to be ready and available to address the presence of evil spirits that may oppress believers or control unbelievers. As we are given discernment to expose them we, in the power of Jesus Name have the authority to eradicate them. The Word itself expresses that "the Holy Spirit and fire" be deliberately linked, because fire speaks of both purifying and purposeful power over every manifestation of evil.

In Dr. Quentin McGhee's assertion that there is "a great contrast between the baptisms of John and Jesus…John promised that Jesus would baptize, not in water, but in fire…In 1665 the city of London, England suffered from a terrible disease. Thousands died. The disease was hiding and growing in buildings. Washing walls and floors did not get rid of the plague. In the year that followed, a great fire burned the city. London was baptized in fire! The flames destroyed the deadly disease. Fire accomplished what water could not do."[2] It was because of this anticipated and pervasive effectiveness of the Spirit's fire that would prompt Jesus to declare, "I came to send fire on the earth, and how I wish it were already kindled" (Lk. 12:49). Now I recognize that this verse has been interpreted several different ways but, I am in total agreement with what F. F. Bruce wrote in *The Hard Sayings of Jesus*: "It is more satisfactory to take these words as the expression of a longing for an outpouring of the Spirit in power the like of which had not yet been seen."[3] Bruce also links the idea of fire in this passage with the usage of fire in John's description of Jesus' ministry and work.[4] Bruce connects the significance of fire in Luke 12:49 with the fire of the Spirit in Acts 2:3-4 on the day of Pentecost: "The fire was there in Jesus' ministry, but the earth had not yet caught fire. One day it would catch fire in earnest, with the descent of the Holy Spirit at Pentecost."[5] The Church is in want of a fresh awakening to the purging, liberating and healing power of the Spirit's fire. And I affirm with all the strength within me that the best delivery system for casting that fire afresh upon the earth is by and through the speaking of the Word. That's what is so needed today!

My concerns are not in opposition to higher education and training, for they are both useful instruments to convey the Word, when subordinated to the Holy Spirit. My admonition is that, as preacher's we would do well not to educate the mind too far ahead of nurturing the spirit. The advertisement for education that says "the mind is a terrible thing to waste" is certainly a profitable reminder. However, our enlightenment tendency to fill the mind with ideas and information at the expense of the training of our spirit by the Word, is an error we can ill afford. When the Church becomes overly concerned with training the intellect with the rational disciplines of a humanistic and naturalistic worldview at the expense of experiencing the supernatural works of the Spirit within a biblical worldview, we have entered the arena of wrong methodology. Stated another way, as believers we have often jumped into the fray without laying hold of the proper weapons beforehand.

The last passage of scriptural text is found in I Kings 18:24. Here is the well-known story of Elijah who takes on the prophets of Baal on Mount Carmel. Although this text is from the Old Testament, it addresses the spiritual response and the ministry expectation that we must appropriate today if we would be heirs of the victorious message of the Bible against all the enemies of God's people. Examining the religion and worship of Baal provides an excellent example of two worldviews that oppress our modern American culture. Within the very structure of this ancient religion, one finds the foundations for two of the most dangerous and destructive paradigms presently at work in contemporary America. Oddly enough, when lined up amidst the spectrum of worldviews, they lay at opposite ends one from the other and yet they vie for the confused hearts and minds within our post-Christian society. The two false views I'm referring to are animism and naturalism. The religion of Baal displayed aspects of animism in the form of spirit worship and witchcraft, yet also portrayed a very primitive form of naturalism being a religion based on the cycles and worship of nature.

The priests of Baal sought to control people through sorcery or prophesies whose source was demon spirits, and also deified nature through sexual and fleshly depravity. These two worldview perspectives are actually contradictory paradigms within that one religion. Satan used this one false religion in an attempt to satisfy two dominate aspects of man's fallen nature, namely our desire for cosmic control and our tendency to reduce the supernatural to the natural. In reality these two belief systems are opposite in their philosophical premises, but for years these two dark forces co-mingled and conspired to keep Israel in spiritual bondage and darkness. Both worldviews operating in one false religion were Satan's means of preventing Israel from living out both its moral righteousness and its supernatural vitality.

These are also the two most powerful contradictory worldviews struggling for the soul of America. The spread of our modern western secularism (a combination of materialism, humanism and naturalism) has left us with a spiritual vacuum that lured us into our current postmodern relativism (a conglomeration of many religious and philosophical streams to create our present state, of what I call, cultural polytheism). America has been infiltrated by a contemporary version of Baal worship with its vast array of prophets, priests, mystical gurus and liberal academics.

The Old Testament prophet was sounding out the Spirit-endued declaration of Kingdom expectation when he was faced with all the antics and forms of their demonic religion. He encouraged them "Then you call on the name of your gods, and I will call on the name of the Lord; and the God who answers by fire, He is God." (I Kings 18:24). With the terms of engagement having been established, the pagan priests did what they knew to do. From morning till evening they vented their animistic mantras and chanted their hymns that "nature is all there is, was or ever shall be" (this was Carl Sagan's scientific anthem to declare his philosophical naturalism). Finally as the day was drawing to a close, Elijah simply stepped up to his pulpit in front of the repaired altar of God (The Cross) and the people (The Church) and expected God to pour out His glory by moving upon the situation in supernatural demonstration (The Holy Spirit).

The challenge today is the same as in those days of old. I believe that God is calling for pastors, missionaries and teachers to come forth in that same spirit and faith of Elijah, and believe for the fire of God to fall afresh. I am not referring to the fire of judgment that James and John wanted to call down upon the Samaritan village for their rejection of Christ (Lk. 9:54). Rather, I am referring to the renewing and refreshing fire of Pentecostal witness that converted three thousand souls in Acts 2 and registered numerous supernatural signs and wonders .

The greatest flames of compassion can be seen in the passion of proclamation that carries the force of liberating grace, because it is the Word alone that is able to set persons free from all that oppresses. Note that Elijah simply called out to God to manifest His glory to the people, so that the true God would be validated and that the hearts of the people would be drawn back to Him. Then suddenly, "the fire of the Lord fell" (I Kings 18:38) from heaven and consumed all things earthly. God manifested Himself with such power and might that the people recognized His greatness and responded with exuberant praise and acclamation, "The Lord, He is God!" (I Kings 18:39). I am convinced that as preachers and saints of God begin to move and minister in this kind of Spirit-directed fire, America too will experience a return to the true Lord and Savior Jesus Christ. People caught in the web of Satan's lies deserve the truth that will bring life-changing deliverance. Atheist and animist alike have a right to hear and see the Gospel that comes with demonstrations of "the Holy Spirit and fire."

SUPPORTING QUOTES RELATED TO THE TEXT

"Relegated to the realm of historians, biblical interpretation becomes separated from the use of the Scriptures within and for the life the church. Modern preaching is left to develop under the watchful, regulative eye of the professional exegete/historian...the preacher is to find an appropriate application for the biblical text once the specialist has excavated the text singular meaning."[6]

"The preacher must first address one audience in preparation for the sermon—the objective, abstract, rational, disembodied human being—to find the meaning of the text and then move to a second audience, the very particular, located, concrete life of a congregation and individuals within it for the rhetorical presentation of this previously established meaning."[7]

"The word *fire* is symbolic of the Holy Spirit. Fire purifies, consumes, and transforms. Under the power of the Holy

Spirit we may fall, tremble, or laugh, but none of these manifestations will change us. God does move in these ways, but we must not set our eyes on such manifestations. What will *change* our lives is the fire that fell on Pentecost, the same fire that was evident in the lives of the apostles."[8]

"When Annacondia opened the door, I said to him immediately, 'Brother, I've come to pray with you. I want the spiritual fire that you have.'"[9]

"On one occasion a young Buddhist lady sat opposite me in the square. She had raised a sort of altar with a lighted candle, and when I rebuked the demon that held her subject to his will, she suddenly fell backward—candle and all! God put the power of her idols to shame."[10]

"Even so, something draws the deeper part of us almost irresistibly to the ragged-edged real, even over the sleek, smooth, and stunning."[11]

"Anyway, you've probably found it hard to feel superior to animals about your anatomy when so many of them are faster and stronger than you. That leaves fire. And yes, indeed, although you can teach a chimpanzee to smoke, no species of wild animals uses fire. But all human societies do and have since time immemorial. Indeed, it is obvious that all of the technology you take for granted today, from cars and computers to plastics and modern media, began with fire."[12]

"The symbol of the Spirit is not only wind but fire. Some men are so aflame with the Spirit that to draw near to them is to be where the sparks fall. A Christian congregation is a failure if, in its midst, the Spirit does not break out into flame and fire."[13]

"If you want to see miracles...spread the gospel. Miracles tend to happen when you're presenting Christ to people... In the Zhoukou district of China, a rather new Christian began evangelizing on the streets, While he was preaching, a man came up and started swearing at him and beating him with a heavy stick. The Preacher began praying, 'Lord, you have to answer my prayer now, or I'm going home!' Then he had a thought. 'In Jesus' name, I *bind* you!' he declared. Immediately, his attacker collapsed into a kneeling position and *was unable to move.* Soon, five of his relatives came and tried to lift him up—with no success. The young preacher, now emboldened, warned, 'He is bound. If I don't pray for him, the only way you can move him is to hoist him into a truck.' At this, the crowd began shouting, 'Please let him free!' So the preacher relented. 'All right, in Jesus' name, get up.' The man quickly stood. Many in that village believed in Jesus because of this wonder.' Chinese Christians never set out to do miracles. They insist that miracles just happen in the course of evangelizing."[14]

"First let me say that when the power of the Holy Spirit is upon a person or a church you can no more stifle the manifestations without quenching the power of the Spirit than you can shut off all air from a fire without extinguishing it."[15]

"The truth is that Pentecostalism was, and is, as the sociologist David Martin says, 'a potent mixture of the pre-modern and the postmodern, of the preliterate and the postliterate, of the fiesta and the encounter group.' Little wonder that, once having fallen on the city of Angels, the fire would spread to the cities of the earth."[16]

QUESTIONS RELATED TO THE TEXT

1. In respect to the fire on the roof in my narrative section, was it more likely that the children were playing a prank, they simply imagined it all, or could there have been an actual fire that went out on its own?

2. Is it fair to say that when it comes to miraculous events, there will always be alternative explanation?

3. When telling a personal story, what is the preacher's moral obligation to keep it as accurate as possible?

4. How much is our truthfulness related to our sense of authenticity, especially when it comes to our mandate to preach?

5. How might a gradual embracing of the Liberal theology affect our confidence in the preaching of the Word and of our expectations of its supernatural results?

6. In what ways do the premises of enlightenment rationalism still diminish the modern desire for experiencing the Spirit and for proclamation under the anointing of the Spirit?

7. In your honest opinion is it a stretch to identify two worldviews of animism and naturalism within the primitive religion of Baalism?

8. What is the appropriate balance between seeking the spiritual presence of the Spirit and requiring His physical manifestations?

CHAPTER NINE

PSALMS 107:20; MATTHEW 4:4, 8:16; JOHN 1:1; 15:20

THE DNA OF THE WORD

A NARRATIVE RESPONSE TO THE TEXT

Let me express here some of the questions you may be entertaining, like, why should we as Bible believers have so much confidence in preaching as God's primary method of communicating His Word and works? After all isn't this particular medium of idea exposure being more and more demeaned by the world we live in? Not only is our western culture becoming more resistant, but even the Church that gave birth to the sermon and has continued to nurture its use for thousands of years has begun to disregard its significance. Hasn't preaching had its day? Hasn't preaching been tried long enough and been found wanting? Hasn't technology and multimedia approach made verbal proclamation an antiquated conundrum?

I believe that any method of communication can and should be enlisted to engage the mind of man with Christ's Word. In fact, it was just such questions that instigated a thoughtful and introspective dialogue with God a couple of years ago. It was that prayerful enquiry to God that prompted what I consider to be a divinely given insight about the Bible as the Word of God and all forms of verbally communicating its content.

I have always said and believed the Bible to be God's Word, except for those few years of liberal theology back in my early days of seminary training. However, because we live in such a skeptical age, in regard to both the Bible and preaching, I wish to record my perceptions of this ongoing dialogue with God in this text's final chapter. My discussion with the Lord was not to question the validity of the Bible as being God's Word, but more along the lines of why we believe it to be so. Now I knew all the catch phrases, all the traditional responses and all the orthodox rationales for accepting the Bible as the Word of God, but I was bold enough to press for more understanding. I realized that perhaps I was being presumptuous and yet I believed that even my inquiry was an appropriate one and worth pursuing. Therefore, I pressed my respectful probing with an honest desire to communicate the doctrine of divine inspiration in a way that was more relevant and understandable to the contemporary mind. The following is a paraphrased report of what I believe to be an illuminating explanation of why we must embrace all expressions of God's Word, whether it's presented in its written or spoken forms.

To answer the question about why and how we might better appreciate the Word of God, especially in its written and verbal forms, it seemed as though the Lord began quizzing me about what might have been the first expression of His Word. I invited the Holy Spirit to direct me and my thoughts as we began to journey back in time as we humans understand time. Immediately, I felt the Lord was prompting me to discover the answer to His question by pointing further into the past than the eyes of man can see. Then it dawned on me that the Spirit was referring to His *Eternal Word*; that Word which existed even before time and space; that Word that even preceded the Word that spoke the universe into existence and told it to be. I was intrigued by that thought, so in my limited human thinking, I wondered and even reasoned that this *Eternal Word* may have been the very language of heaven before time began. Perhaps this is the language of heaven and of angels (1 Co. 13:1) that is and will be spoken throughout heaven's realm, although only heaven knows that for sure. Since this *Eternal Word* or language is beyond the human and temporal grasp, it is still cloaked in mystery (1 Co.14:2). This may have been what the Lord was expressing to Moses when He informed him that "The secret things belong to the Lord our God, but those things which are revealed belong to us and to our children forever, that we may do all the words of this law" (Deut. 29:29).

The *Eternal Word* from God reminds us that for all His words of revelation, there will always be things that we will never be able to wrap our minds around. It is a part of God's omniscient character to keep a few secrets protected from human ego that thinks it is its own creator, as is preached by philosophical naturalism and atheistic science. Only in eternity future will we be able to receive our clearest understanding of this *Eternal Word* (I Co. 13:12). There will never be any Word quite like this *Eternal Word*, for it is the language of God and of heaven from before time began. It is not a language that belongs to earth, except by divine generosity and unveiling, for it is His word that belongs essentially to infinity. The *Eternal Word* is unique because it is the source and destiny of all God's words and the energy for all His other speaking.

At that point I felt the Lord reminding me that at creation, He uttered His next great expression of His Word and that was His wonderful *Creative Word*. By this Word, Christ spoke the worlds into being. He spoke and nothingness took shape into something. In the words of philosophy one could say that is why "there is something rather than nothing." With the beginning of time, space, energy and matter the *Eternal Word* of heaven became the *Creative Word* on earth. Only then did time begin its linear march throughout the temporal dispensations and historic ages. It was the *Creative Word* that introduced the process of God's divine revelation to mankind. The *Eternal Word* wrapped in mystery became the unveiled *Creative Word* as Christ unwrapped what always was, is and shall ever be. For the first time we beheld His true triune nature (Gen. 1:26) as Christ (Col. 1:15-17) called forth the universe out of nothing at the will of the Father and by the agency of the Spirit (1 Jn. 5:7-8). Without this *Creative Word* coming to be, the *Eternal Word* would have remained as unknown as the mysteries of the sea. With the divine intervention of God at creation, God's Word would no longer be hidden as heaven's secret, but would now show forth His limitless delight, boundless depth and extravagant desire for mankind.

Again, as God spoke to Moses, "For this commandment which I command you today is not too mysterious for you, nor is it far off. It is not in heaven, that you should say, Who will ascend into heaven for us and bring it to us, that we may hear it and do it" (Deut. 30:11-12). Starting with the *Creative Word*, mankind took on a measure of responsibility before God, for God's will was no longer beyond man's capacity to understand. Of course, mankind's fall would disrupt and circumvent that human capacity, but not destroy it completely. We must remember that when God revealed the Torah to Moses, that event also included His first unveiling of the Creation's account. In Genesis, chapters one and two record the moment when Christ first exhaled that first *Creative Word* and all of life began to pulsate with His life and reflect His light. This Word alone produced the miracle of space and time within the cosmic order and resulted in the matter and energy of divine light. There will never be any Word quite like this *Creative Word* for it was the first Word to enter our realm of human comprehension as it was always meant to be.

Thanks to the grace and genius of our God, the *Creative Word* would not be the last Word. Those light waves and particles would not only begin the progression of historical time and set in motion an ever expanding universe, but God's linguistic character would send forth another living word. Jehovah or *Yahweh* was just getting started because He had so much more to say. As I reflected back over the broad spectrum of all the epochs of time it seemed most appropriate to identify the next crucial method of divine speech. This particular address would come by way of a rather strange blending of both the human and divine and would foretell God's predetermined will. It would be heralded from primitive eons past as the *Prophetic Word*. Through this Word, the Spirit would utter both what is and what was yet to be. The prophet breathed in the air that now is, but breathed out what was to be. This was the word that God first employed to communicate His will and thus ventured to entrust that will to men. Whereas the *Creative Word* was spoken directly from God to uncreated matter, the *Prophetic Word* is spoken to the flesh and blood matter of created man; a declaration from God to man, His revelation through a man to men. The *Prophetic Word* becomes God's human vessel for declaring heaven's will. It is His deliberate and sometimes risky exchange for men, to men. This word represents God's determined purpose to communicate His heart from person to person. It is His designed plan to confront earth's wayward spin by heavens upward call; to bring into vertical alignment our downward spiral. The fact that God entrusted this perfect word to flawed and imperfect vessels makes it special and unique from all God's other forms of speaking.

The *Prophetic Word* represents God's heart, for it first reveals His desire to involve fallen mankind into His creative intentions. Through the *Prophetic Word,* the Spirit speaks the Father's purposes to His chosen servants, who are then compelled to declare that will and testament to others. The very existence of this word ought to really confound our minds when we consider its distinctive character. Just think about this, God was choosing to let us in on those mysteries that only He knew. The *Creative Word* was not adequate to the task, because it was pronounced before there was any human audience. However, the *Prophetic Word* was God's first revelational Word to man, by man, for man. It is for that reason that the *Prophetic Word* would have to be progressive in nature, because man in his now fallen condition, could only receive a divine word incrementally. Therefore, God's *Prophetic Word* would have to be "here a little, there a little" (Isa. 28:10). In other words it would have to come in stages, or from "glory to glory" (2 Cor. 3:18). This developmental nature of the *Prophetic Word* exists because of man's comprehension limitations, his human boundaries and his fallen cognitive capabilities. What a wonderful and generous God we serve. His *Creative Word* was awesome, but it was declared before there was an audience to appreciate, acknowledge or applaud it. However, the *Prophetic Word* provided the means whereby mankind would become privy to a portion of the divine mind and wisdom. What trust! What grace! What love!

I continued to ponder within myself the grandness of His generosity, what could be greater than that? One might appropriately consider that with God's devising such a vertical and horizontal means of communication, He may then have been willing to retire into silence, except for man's continued tendency to deny, disregard and disobey even the words of His prophetic servants. Mankind still labored under deception's weight of self godhood audibly hearing God's words, but remaining unwilling to respond or appreciate them. Therefore, continuing in the great legacy and spirit of the *Prophetic Word*, the Holy Spirit gave birth to the Word whose dimensions would obliterate any boundaries to His infinite grace or mankind's finite limits. This Word would be known in time and extended into eternity future as the *Incarnate Word*. Within this Word, Father God wrapped up a piece of Himself and delivered His son Jesus through the womb of flesh, bone, sinew and blood. Now, the Father no longer had to speak a Word through just a man, but as the Living Word He become a man, that He might be the Word living and speaking the Word (John 1:1-5).

Jesus alone is the Word who spoke the Word and that's what it meant to be the *Incarnate Word*. In Christ the Word, the splendor of God could be both heard and seen. God could be directly heard because when Jesus spoke, His words were formed by the same *ruah* or breath of the Spirit, that formed the words of primal creation, and sparked the first flickers of life in the creature called man. That's why the *Incarnate Word* could speak nothing that did not bring life, light and wonder for He was both "grace and truth"

(John 1:14). The *Incarnate Word* knew no limits except those He chose, in submission to His Father (Phil. 2:6-11). This Word, though born of woman (Gal. 4:4), was conceived by the Spirit (Mt. 1:20) and therefore carried in His genetic inheritance the very essence, or one might say, the very DNA of His true heavenly Father.

He was God clothed in sinless human flesh. He was not man who became God, nor did His human nature take on divine nature. Rather, He was God taking on human, yet sinless nature. He became what we are so that we might become what He is. Only the wonderful *Prophetic Word* could have both foreseen this reality and foretold it. Only the *Incarnate Word* could have reflected and fulfilled it. Only the *Written Word* could have preserved and recorded it and only the *Preached Word* is endowed with the grace to promote and proclaim it. Only those who give ear and heart to the *Incarnate Word* have access or permission to hear and appropriate all the other expressions of God's Word. The Church's mandate is to continue both to reflect and affirm this *Incarnate Word* and to move in its same miracle flow and creative energy. The *Incarnate Word* is most unique because He alone speaks of our triune God's essential character as love. He speaks of the all encompassing Father's love; a love so profound that He would entrust His only begotten son to a world still under the rule of darkness. He speaks of the love of the Son who would make Himself vulnerable to the hatred of those dark forces in order to break their chains of destruction. He speaks of the love of the Spirit that made possible the triumph of the Son in the very midst of that darkness.

It is difficult to cease speaking about the importance of the *Incarnate Word*, for Christ is that Word to which all other divine Words point to, converge in, rest upon and radiate from. This Word is the vortex to which all other God-speech is drawn and the matrix from which all God's speaking flows. Because of the very nature of the *Incarnate Word* God could continue to speak, and so we must also continue His story. God had uttered His ultimate Word in the *Incarnate Word*, but not His exhaustive Word. The *Incarnate Word* was, and will always be God's most crucial Word to the world, but this would not be His last word. To complete His divine plan and fulfill His divine purpose, Christ needed to deliver yet another word. I refer to this as His *Kingdom Word*. It would be during His earthly ministry that Christ translated the *Incarnate Word* into the *Kingdom Word* which He called the Gospel of the Kingdom. This would become His Word of triumph by the Spirit, as He bore witness to both the awesome words and mighty wonders of God. It was this Word which would continue to work through His Church, His new creation of redeemed mankind after Pentecost. Since Christ was temporarily silenced by man in being nailed to the cross, the *Kingdom Word* would show that the *Incarnate Word* would still have the last Word. After the Resurrection, the world and the rulers of darkness would realize that this *Kingdom Word* had the same dynamic force as did the *Incarnate Word*. In fact, as this *Kingdom Word* was proclaimed, its energy rippled outward and its effects grew stronger as the Church was faithful to speak it (Acts 2:41; 4:31; 6:7; 8:4).

The effects of the *Kingdom Word* were felt during the ministry of the *Incarnate Word*, but too few took appropriate notice; "He was sent to His own but they did not recognize Him" (Jn. 1:11); but, when the explosion took place at His Resurrection all the way to the pit of hell the blast was darkness shattering and the radiation light of new life broke loose; it was like another "Big Bang" from which emerged His new creation of redemptive hope along with new creation prospects for planet earth. It was as if the ever-expanding universe continued on its orderly path, but now its movement and course had been set back on track toward its intended destiny, or what the New Testament calls the *eschaton*. With atomic yet invisible force, the resurrected Christ established His Kingdom upon the earth and then empowered its new citizens of that Kingdom with His truth and authority to proclaim this new *Kingdom Word*. As the earth had been "fine tuned" to accommodate the natural order, it now began to be "fine-tuned" to explore life in the Spirit, bringing the life of the empowerment to the Church. This *Kingdom Word* carries within itself its own unique dynamic in that it represents elements of both the present and the future, or the now and the not yet. This *Kingdom Word* speaks of what God has done, what Christ is doing and what the Spirit is drawing us toward. It is the Word of His power that is just waiting to be unleashed upon the world with magnum force.

For this *Kingdom Word* to be disseminated throughout the nations and cultures of the earth, it would require another spiritual metamorphosis. The *Kingdom Word* would need to be transcribed into the *Written Word*, by passing the test of language, so that every ethnic grouping might have its very own copied and encoded expression of the *Kingdom Word* translated into its own language. This *Written Word* while first expressed as spoken word needed the accuracy of its content to be transcribed for posterity into all languages, for every generation and for all peoples. This Word was too great and too awesome to be localized or confined to a particular language, people or nation.

The *Written Word* has passed the test of time and the attacks of all its critics because it was recognized and then canonized as God's own Word. This *Written Word* has ever served as a reminder to God's people, that its message is their missional mandate, and therein stands its grand uniqueness. How excellent is this *Written Word*, for by its endless transmissions and translations, it has traveled by every means possible, and to every known port around the globe, for such was its divine destiny. This *Written Word* gives us a standard from which to navigate on the open sea of human ideas, philosophies of men and multi-cultural worldviews. Without this expression of God's Word, we would be adrift on the treacherous waves of human opinion, finite thinking, faulty worldviews, and perverted cultures. In its written form, the Word of God fulfills both an objective standard for truth and a subjective experience of that truth. This is the meaning of Peter's comment " that no prophesy of Scripture is of any private interpretation…but holy men of God spoke as they were moved by the Holy Spirit" (2 Pet. 1:20-21).

Those who hold to the writings of the *Quran* are usually quick to condescend to any translation of their holy text and declare that its true beauty and authority lies in its original *Arabic* rendering. We who hold to the Bible as the only inspired and *Written Word* of God respond quite differently. Our Bible carries the same authority, grace and truthfulness, no matter what language it is clothed in. Its diversity of written forms merely represents its 'external robe,' which does not affect its inner coherency. The Bible's multiplicity of translations adds, not to its accuracy but to its beauty, grace and authority. Since God has left a deposit of His general revelation of Himself in every human culture (Acts 17:22-30; Rom. 1:20-21), all cultural languages can become a worthy vehicle of God's *Written Word,* for His Holy Spirit continues to superintend its many translations.

My personal concern however, is with we who profess to believe the Bible, but determine to maintain a skeptical mind. Why would one need to question the Bible's authenticity as God's Word, if he or she can believe in an omnipotent Holy Spirit who watches over every aspect of its transmission? If the Spirit has all the attributes of deity, then why would it be considered too hard a task for Him to oversee its continued transcriptions and translations? Can you believe in God? Then you should have no problem in believing that He can protect and defend every aspect of His Word, whatever the form. Again it may be asked, why should, or how can we, trust the Bible as God's *Written Word* since men were involved in its initial writing and later copying? I repeat for emphasis, the *Written Word* is a wonder to behold, for it like all other forms of God's speaking, share a common DNA. The *Written Word* contains the same genetic code as does the *Kingdom Word,* which was proclaimed by the *Incarnate Word.* Therefore, to doubt any expression of the Word is to doubt all, and to question the validity of any of God's words, is to question the Holy Spirit that gave birth to all of them. So, if we are going to start the process of doubt, where will it cease? If one spends his time questioning another's last will and testament, is he not questioning the veracity of the one who willed it or the one who wrote it?

Only one more word is needed to take us through to the completed pilgrimage of God's Word, and that is the *Preached Word* (including all verbal witness). While it would be difficult to ascertain which has received the greatest amount of abuse over the centuries, the *Written Word* or the *Preached Word*, I would say that the latter has probably received the greater amount of repudiation. This is especially true in our day and time, and this is perhaps the reason that it has been the *Preached Word* that has been the focus of this volume. This particular expression of the Word is unique among all God's word forms because it alone seems most vulnerable to human frailty and secular indictment. This is because the world's attacks center on their own judging of the ineffectiveness of the preacher. The world's negative reactions are also based upon a faulty assessment of the confronting message it needs to hear. Human response is often inappropriate since preaching is not meant to be entertainment nor simply to address the wants or desires of an audience. On the other hand, their negative reaction can be a useful barometer if preaching is not meeting the genuine needs of the whole person. If preaching is not addressing man's spirit, soul and body, it is not fulfilling its biblical purpose.

The *Preached Word* is truly a unique expression of God's Word, because through it God has made Himself most open to man's manipulation. Because of human weaknesses, we preachers can brutalize and mutilate the *Preached Word* in any number of ways and we often do. We can legalize it, spiritualize it, secularize it, individualize it, scrutinize it and generally terrorize the biblical text to death. I have often been guilty myself of such torturing of the good Word of God on the rack of sermon preparation. All of this is true and yet, none of this gives a believer one iota of an excuse or permit a scrap of rationale to diminish, dilute or dismiss the *Preached Word* of God, if indeed it is the Word of God being proclaimed.

The messenger of any aspect of God's Word should be authentic, holy, diligent and skillful, but the preacher is not the central issue. If the *Preached Word* of God is going forth, we must have the expectation that it will do its work because of what it is. Our expectations of His Word ought to take a gigantic leap upward in the voting polls of God's people, because it too shares the same DNA with the *Written Word*. The *Preached Word* is of the same authoritative essence as all the other divine methods of God's speaking. To trace this truth further, and again I repeat for emphasis' sake, we affirm that the *Written Word* has in common, the same DNA with the *Kingdom Word* and the *Kingdom Word* carries in its information code, the same DNA as the *Incarnate Word* who was and is the King of kings and Lord of lords.

To press this idea to its ultimate conclusion, The *Incarnate Word* as John's divine *Logos* had its origins also in the *Prophetic Word*, and in the initial explosion of God's beginning *Creative Word* that first made the divine pronouncement "Let there be" (Genesis chapter One). Finally, the Word that first caused the natural ordering of the universe as the divine "First Cause" exerted its expanding energy of creative force. Every particle and sub-particle of matter in the cosmos was thrust into orbiting space by that *Creative Word* which drew its release from the hidden energy of God's mysterious *Eternal Word*.

This whole narrative section is one preacher's pursuit to discover the DNA of preaching (or of the spoken word) and to answer the question regarding why I hold to such a high view of both the words of scripture and the preaching event, and why the Church ought also to arrive at the same conclusion. It is for the survival of the world and the good of all nations for which Christ has made us, the Church, responsible to love, proclaim and to bear witness to its immeasurable worth and unsearchable riches.

AN EXPOSITIONAL INQUIRY INTO THE TEXT
Ps. 107: 20; Matthew 4:4; 8:16; John 1:1; 15:20

The first passage I want to look at is found in Psalm 107:20. It was this verse that first prompted my narrative search into the potential significance and multiple meanings of the Word of God. One day a couple of years ago, I was reading, "He sent His word and healed them." And those simple words encouraged me to ask, what seemed at the time, a nonsensical question. I asked myself, to which or to what word was the psalmist referring? As I repeated the words "He sent His word and healed them," I was tremendously moved by both key ideas in the text, found in the terms "word" and "healing". I was immediately awed by the combination of those two simple words.

That phrase "He sent His word and healed them" shows how the Old Testament can break through with revelation that makes it seem more like it came from the New Testament. Again my mind probed, wanting to grasp which aspect in these words the writer was making such power claims? When the author spoke of the "word", was he implying the word of the Bible, the Gospels, the prophets or John's *Logos*? Then it occurred to me that the psalmist was perhaps speaking inclusively. I believe that he was suggesting that when God's Word goes forth, it has supernatural power, whatever its mode of expression. God's Word has dynamic and miraculous properties, whether it is His *Eternal, Creative, Prophetic, Incarnate, Kingdom, Written, or Preached Word*. The next question formed itself into, why or how this would be so? It is because they all share the same spiritual or supernatural DNA. Although each expression of God's Word fulfills a unique and distinct purpose and function, they all contain the same Spirit-given divine essence.

Coming to recognize the awesome variety in which God communicates His same message, greatly enhanced for me the significance of Psalm 107:20. Just one further note on this text has to do with our response of thanksgiving for God's "wonderful works" (verses 8, 15, 21, and 31). This follows properly with the theme that God's Word works no matter what form or shape it takes. "The wonderful works" of God are the natural outcome of His grace-filled Word and our believing response. I submit that this marvelous phrase in this passage certainly refers to the *Preached Word* as much as it refers to any other means of divine speaking. The Bible confirms throughout the New Testament that preaching produced healing on a consistent basis (Mk. 1:21-27, 39, 40-42) and that healing could manifest itself in man's spirit, mind, emotions or body.

The second text for this chapter is found in Matthew 4:4 and relates to Jesus' first reply to Satan in the wilderness temptations. In biblical thought, the wilderness was a place where evil spirits or demonic forces made their preferred habitation. One might say it was the place where the Word of God was not welcomed and yet this is precisely the location where the Spirit drove the *Incarnate Word* to face the devil (Mt. 4:1). When tempted to "command that these stones become bread" (Mt. 4:3), Jesus answers, "It is written, 'Man shall not live by bread alone, but by every word that proceeds from the mouth of God'" (Mt. 4:4).

While there is much that could be expounded on here, my emphasis is upon Jesus' stress that His followers are expected to live by "every word" that God speaks. To me this is another clear indication of the diversity of ways in which God has and does communicate His Word. Although we may find the method of God's speaking we best respond to, because all expressions of God language represent His truth, we do not have the right as believers, to accept one form of God speech and not another, for they all proceed "from the mouth of God" (Mt. 4:4). This particular verse relates to Jesus' high view of the *Written Word* even from the Old

Testament, since He is quoting from Deuteronomy 8:3. Jesus' use of this verse is a reminder that Israel had been fed by the *Creative Word* or miracle manna, but they must also trust the *Prophetic Word* by walking in faithful adherence to His law.

Whatever diverse shape the Word may take, it becomes a word-event with power because it comes from the mouth of God. There are biblical terms for "word" in both the Old Testament (*dabar*) and the New Testament (*rhema*) that actually carry the dual meaning of both a word being spoken and an event occurring, and is called the word-event formula.[1] Even though it is well understood that preaching today always comes through the weak vessel of a flesh and blood preacher, we of Western culture upbringing, have too long allowed the human component to diminish our confidence in the *Preached Word* as still being the Word of God and containing the same DNA as all God's other forms of expression. We as Americans should especially repent for the way we have allowed the erosion of preaching, by focusing on the bearer of the Word rather than on the power of the Word. The vessel bringing the Word will never measure up to the task of being a worthy container. We are all indeed, like those to whom we speak; we are all pots of clay, but the point of focus should be not on the externals, but on the glorious treasure within (2 Cor. 4:7).

The third text to examine more closely here is found in Matthew 8:16. Chapter eight reports five major miracle events covering Jesus' power over severe disease, a disabling affliction, a common fever, a demonic control over the elements and the casting out of fierce and destructive demons. Jesus was no doubt following the will and direction of the Father in the power of the Holy Spirit (Jn. 12: 50; 14:10) as He always did. For miracles to happen, it was needful to have an environment of faith expectancy for the release of supernatural power (Lk. 5:17). What seems most significant to me is that it was Jesus' proclamation and witness to the Word that instigated the divine set-up for miracles to occur. It seems to me that the recorded signs and wonders in chapter eight were so prolific because chapter seven ends with this explanation "that the people were astonished at His teaching, for He taught them as one having authority, and not as the scribes" (Mt. 7:28-29). The working power of the Holy Spirit is often premised by the authoritative power of the Word. I believe Matthew is definitely making the connection between the healing Presence and Word proclamation when he writes, "When evening had come, they brought to Him many who were demon-possessed. And He cast out the spirits with a word, and healed all who were sick" (Mt. 8:16). What a powerful statement about the laden power dynamic that is deposited in the Word.

But which Word? To what Word does the *Written Word* point? The *Preached Word* may have been the usual method of dissemination, but to the Jewish mind when supernatural energy was displayed, it was often identified with the *Prophetic Word* being fulfilled (Mt. 8:17). The ultimate reference point is Jesus, the *Incarnate Word* or *Logos* and when this term is used, it doesn't usually distinguish between the word spoken and the result that it brings about. William D. Mounce affirms: "*Logos* means 'word, message, report' and sometimes even 'deed'"[2] The term *Logos* represents both cause and effect. Therefore, does it really matter which form of God's Word is being referred to, when they all exhibit the same commonality of life, light and energy, and all come from the same source of the *Eternal Word?*

It is an astounding concept that when it comes to all God's speaking, all God's Words or all expressions of God language, there has been written into its informational code or design, the very force that produces what it has announced. Isn't that the very intent of the prophet Isaiah when he declared, "For as the rain comes down, and the snow from heaven, and do not return there, but water the earth, and make it bring forth and bud, that it may give seed to the sower and bread to the eater, so shall My word be that goes forth from my mouth; It shall not return to Me void, but it shall accomplish what I please, and it shall prosper in the thing for which I sent it" (Isa. 55:10-11)? When Isaiah spoke the *Prophetic Word* concerning the yet to come Jesus, he announced that "The Spirit of the Lord God is upon Me, because the Lord has anointed Me to preach good tidings to the poor; He has sent Me to heal the brokenhearted, to proclaim liberty to the captives, and the opening of the prison to those who are bound; to proclaim the acceptable year of the Lord" (Isa. 61:1-2). Jesus reiterated this passage as His coronation motif or mission statement. He embraced it as His *Kingdom Word* being fulfilled in Himself in a manner referred to, as the Gospel of the Kingdom (Lk. 4:18-19).

The final text, John 15:20, makes a direct connection between His words and ours. He comments to His disciples that "If they kept My word, they will keep yours also." First, I believe that Jesus is drawing a parallel between His *Kingdom Word* and the Church's *Preached Word*. Second, He is giving the Church its greatest challenge and that challenge is for us to demonstrate the same results that He did. This challenge has always been a battle for the Church, but according to Jesus, not an impossible or inappropriate expectation (Jn. 14:12). I believe that the Church's greatest mandate for today is no different from what it has always been and that is "to preach the Word" (2 Tim. 4:2).

But, there is also that accompanying call to those who would preach or bear witness to the Word today. The admonition given by the author of Hebrews is that we must not fall away from the living God into unbelief as did Israel of Old (Heb. 3:12). It was their low confidence and lack of faith expectency, not only in the *Prophetic Word*, but also in the *Preached Word* that led to their spiritual demise. It is recorded: "For indeed the gospel was preached to us as well as to them; but the word which they heard did not profit them, not being mixed with faith in those who heard it" (Heb. 4:2). Because of the living *Incarnate Word* that dwells within us and the power of the *Kingdom Word* that is near us, we simply must trust the Word to work in us and through us, whatever form it takes.

Praise God, we don't have to emotionally work something up or force God to move. Rather, after speaking the Word our response is to rest and allow God's Word to work. As Hebrews continues, "For he who has entered His rest has ceased from his works as God did from His. Let us therefore be diligent to enter that rest, lest anyone fall according to the same example of disobedience" (Heb. 4:6). The author of Hebrews exclaims, "For the word of God is living and powerful, and sharper than any two-edged sword, piercing even to the division of soul and spirit, and of joints and marrow, and is a discerner of the thoughts and intents of the heart" (Heb. 4:10-12). Whatever form of divine proclamation the writer is acknowledging, it shares in the same divine source.

Our responsibility and privilege, as believers, is simply to trust and expect the Word of God to produce its own results. It is my belief that the next and final spiritual revival (Ps. 119:25,107 and 154) will be one that lasts through the end of time, because it is going to be a revival by way of a new awakening to the power of preaching and witnessing of the Word: "Yet once more I shake not only the earth, but also heaven…the removal of those things that are being shaken, as of things that are made, that the things which cannot be shaken may remain" (Heb. 12:26-27). How do we know that the one remaining unshaken reality is the Word? Jesus, Himself informs us as He reminds His disciples, "Heaven and earth will pass away, but My words will by no means pass away" (Mt. 24:35); a strong and emphatic verse to confirm the eternal nature of God's Word. The next and final revival will be one that prompts the full restoration of God's Word and will therefore, exceed all former times of refreshing. Its impact will rely on no person, but solely on the power of the Word, both written and spoken. My purpose for writing this book is, in fact, to further reinforce the reader's confidence, trust, faith, expectation, and anticipation for every expression of God's Word.

In reminder, all manner of God's communication contains the same informational and transformational DNA, which extends particularly and especially to the arena of preaching, for this is the mode of God's disclosure that has been hardest hit in the last several generations. So "preach the Word" or bear witness to the Word with such power by the Spirit's anointing, that we can say with the apostle Paul, "in mighty signs and wonders, by the power of the Spirit of God, so that from Jerusalem and round about to Illyricum I have fully preached the gospel of Christ" (Rom. 15:19).

When I titled this chapter, "The DNA of Preaching," I was envisioning the idea of the physical make-up of the human cell. My understanding is that DNA is the information code stored in a cell, that directs that cell in becoming what it is genetically programmed to become. It's the cellular blueprint for its growth, development and replication. DNA is the data or message within the cell that guides and controls its very existence and purpose. In other words DNA is information, code, message or word that directs the sequencing for that cell's development. DNA is God's innate recorded language written within every cell of our bodies to release the miracle of God's orderly purpose, direction and oversight of life. It is Christ's sustaining Word and common grace even now at work to make all things coalesce and work together (Col. 1:16-17). For further explanations of the meaning and importance of DNA, see Dr. Henry M. Morris' text, *The Biblical Basis for Modern Science* and Norman L. Geisler's and Frank Turek's volume, *I Don't Have Enough Faith to Be an Atheist* (both books are listed in this chapter's references).[3]

The DNA of preaching in a spiritual sense, is a reference to the life and energy stored in every structure and fiber of God's Word, that is able to produce its intended results. It is biblically proper to use natural language to explicate spiritual reality, as the apostle Paul does in describing the natural and spiritual bodies in 1 Corinthians (1 Co. 15:35-49). It was just recently that I came across the following words written by W. J. Bauer and quoted by Dr. Jack R. Taylor:

"God, an infinite person of infinite power and existence
in and outside time, has created by means of His Word

and through words. We can see evidence of this in every living organism, be it plant or animal. Every living cell has a DNA system which is the 'sine quo non' of its biological life. Life exists only where the 'word system' called DNA is present...The DNA is purely and simply an information system. Meaning in such systems is a function of the sequence of the elements of communication, as the letters in a book, and the nucleotides in the DNA chains...There is no more direct evidence that the method of creation was the spoken Word of God...*That Word is the sole source of our biological life.*"[4]

Preaching's shared DNA, with all the rest of God's speaking, is what gives preaching its significance and speaks of the mutual supernatural life-force coursing through every mode of its expression. Preaching as a means of proclaiming God's Word is but one of the forms of communicating divine information or revelation to mankind; it is involved in that same revelatory process as all the other forms of divine communication that are mentioned in the Bible. It is through the Bible as the *Written Word* that we are made aware of all the other types of God's revelatory Words shown to be His *Eternal Word*, His *Creative Word*, His *Prophetic Word*, His *Incarnate Word*, and His *Preached Word*. One might say that there is a Spirit-encoded symbiotic relationship between all God's ways of disseminating His Word.

I regard John 1:1 to be my central verse, in that it is the *Incarnate Word* that most represents all modes of divine proclamation. Jesus, as the *Logos*, was the physical incarnation and core manifestation of the *Eternal, Creative, Prophetic, Kingdom, Written* and *Preached Word*. Here are other complementary scriptures for your further perusal and personal admonition: Heb. 1:1-3; 2:2-4; Mt. 24:35; Ps. 119:89, 130, 160; 138:2; Rom. 10:14-15; 16:25-26; 1 Cor. 1:20-21; 2:4-5; 2 Cor. 1:19-20; Gal. 3:5; Eph. 6:17; Col. 1:16; 2: 8; Jn. 12:48; 17:17; Mk. 2:2; 12:24; Lk. 4:36; 7:7; 8:49; 13:10-11; 2 Pet. 1:20-21; Rev. 1: 16; 12:10-11; 19:11-13

SUPPORTING QUOTES RELATED TO THE TEXT

"As the leader of the international Human Genome Project, which had labored mightily over more than a decade to reveal this DNA sequence, I stood beside President Bill Clinton in the East Room of the White House… 'Today,' he said, 'we are learning the language in which God created life. We are gaining ever more awe for the complexity, the beauty, and the wonder of God's most divine and sacred gift.'"[5]

"I echoed this sentiment: 'It's a happy day for the world. It is humbling for me, and awe-inspiring, to realize that we have caught the first glimpse of our own instruction book, previously known only to God.'"[6]

"Scholars will recognize *bios* as the Greek word for 'life' (the root word for biology, biochemistry, and so forth), and *logos* as the Greek for 'word.' To many believers, the Word is synonymous with God, as powerfully and poetically expressed in those majestic opening lines of the gospel of John, 'In the beginning was the word, and the Word was with God, and the Word was God' (John 1:1). 'BioLogos' expresses the belief that God is the source of all life and that life expresses the will of God."[7]

"Because information is required for all life processes, it can be stated unequivocally that information is an essential characteristic of all life. All efforts to explain life processes in terms of physics and chemistry only will always be unsuccessful. This is the fundamental problem confronting present-day biology, which is based on evolution."[8]

"The title refers to the first verse of the Gospel written by John: 'In the beginning was the Word….' This book continually emphasizes the fact that information is required for the start of any controlled process, but the information itself is preceded by the prime source of all information. This is exactly what John has written, since 'the Word' refers to the person who is the Prime Cause.'"[9]

"The storage medium is the DNA molecule (deoxyribonucleic acid), which resembles a double helix... and the amount of information is so immense in the case of human DNA that it would stretch from the North Pole to the equator if it was typed on paper, using standard letter sizes. The DNA is structured in such a way that it can be replicated every time a cell divides in two...This replication is so precise, that it can be compared to 280 clerks copying the entire Bible sequentially each one from the previous one, with, at most, one single letter being transposed erroneously in the entire copying process... One cell division lasts from 20-80 minutes, and during this time the entire molecular library, equivalent to one thousand books, is copied correctly."[10]

"The active person at creation was Jesus, 'through whom he made the universe' (Heb. 1:2). Jesus is also the sustainer of the entire creation, 'sustaining all things by his powerful word' (Heb. 1:3). His creative and His sustaining acts are not restricted to matter and energy, but also hold for the information contained in biological systems. We can now conclude (John 1:1-3; Col. 1:16; Heb. 1:2):

__Jesus is the source of all energy,

__Jesus is the source of all matter, and

__Jesus is the source of all biological information."[11]

"If the nature of our universe were not so finely balanced, either it would have expanded so fast that matter would not have had the time to agglomerate into galaxies and stars and planets, in which case the universe would now be a mist of dust and ever weaker radiation, or it would have collapsed in less time than required for galaxies to form. Either way, the universe would today, and forever, be lifeless."[12]

"And then there is life, human life for example. Its chemistry is just as extraordinarily well tuned as is the physics of the cosmos. Our world on both sides of the divide that separates life from lifelessness is filled with wonder."[13]

"What a man can believe depends upon his philosophy, not upon the clock or the century. If a man believes in unalterable natural law, he cannot believe in any miracle in any age. If a man believes in a will behind natural law, he can believe in any miracle in any age."[14]

"But prophetic preaching is about the 'today-ness' of divine reality."[15]

"*Kerygma* is the fashionable word for the message of the Christian pulpit…it is the message of the king's herald…a royal proclamation and the preacher an official messenger."[16]

"Experience must be challenged by Scripture; experience must not challenge Scripture."[17]

"When we bombard the world with the artillery of the gospel, our ammunition is the explosive power of the Holy Spirit."[18]

"It was these signs that drove me to the place where I met the Lord."[19]

"Are we going to proclaim the gospel with wise and persuasive words, or are we going to do it with demonstrations of the power of the Holy Spirit?"[20]

"We are ministers of light, bearers of truth, and heralds of good news to all men everywhere."[21]

"If the above phrase holds even partial truthfulness, how dare we minimize the event of preaching? What gives us a right to denigrate what God exalts as the means of communicating His truth to our generation?"[22]

QUESTIONS RELATED TO THE TEXT

1. What did the title *The DNA of Preaching* indicate to you when you first read it?

2. After reading the full manuscript of this chapter, what is the significance of the title to you now?

3. If you hold to the importance of miracles for today, does it seem biblically appropriate to give the message of Christ priority over His miracles? How should the two be related?

4. What scriptures in this chapter best expressed the theme or subject of its content? Which ones best explained the connection between the different expressions of the Word?

5. Which supporting quotes were most helpful in your understanding and appreciating this chapter's texts?

6. What were your impressions of Dr. Francis S. Collins use of the term *BioLogos*? Does this term offer a viable explanation of creation in your opinion or might there be an alternate term?

CONCLUSION

This volume is about preaching in particular and bearing verbal witness to the Word of God in general, the activity in which I have labored for over fifty years. I consider this God's preeminent method of fulfilling His purposes in the earth and establishing the presence of His kingdom in this world. Also, that preaching or any form of proclamation will only fulfill its divine design if it is accompanied with supernatural signs and wonders (Mk. 16:17-20). Christ's ultimate purpose is, and will always be the completion of the Great Commission, world evangelization, global missions, or whatever phrase best represents Christ's work of reconciling the world back to the Father. In other words preaching the Gospel or bearing witness to Christ's person and work, is the divine strategy for accomplishing the missionary outreach to all peoples who dwell upon this planet.

While the first forty years of my ministry were given to preaching, pastoring and teaching the Gospel of Christ with varying degrees of success, the last twelve years have been directed toward fulfilling my ministry through teaching and preaching on the mission field, or in directly promoting missions on the college campus at North Point Bible College (formally known as Zion Bible College). It is my expectation that whatever years I have before me in ministry will, in some way be related to the missionary enterprise. It is mission's intent that best represents the heart of God and which must therefore occupy the vision and work of the Church. All programs and plans of the Church should be employed for the purpose of fulfilling the missionary mandate of Christ in the power of the Holy Spirit. Missions must no longer be seen as one of many functions in the operations of Church life. In these last days, missions must again be viewed as the Spirit's single-minded intention for the community of faith.

To give an overall perspective to this written work, there are three driving forces that underlie the content of this undertaking. The first two components are preaching or speaking the Word of God and embracing the wonders of the Spirit, while the third is that of focusing upon the missional mandate of Christ. These three categories I believe reflect the intent of Scripture, the triune nature of our God and the core of a New Testament Pentecostal faith; these three driving forces cohere and correspond to complete God's plan for the ages. The best presentation of all three of these essential aspects of the Gospel can best be seen in an actual account reported by one of our missionary educators Dr. Del Tarr:

Years ago, a mighty move of the Holy Spirit in Burkina Faso, West Africa, totally changed my life and convinced me of the power of Pentecost. Missionaries and national pastors had been praying and fasting for weeks for the Spirit's outpouring, because less than a third of the fifteen thousand Christians in the Assemblies of God there had been baptized in the Holy Spirit. Early one morning, Jacques Kabore woke up everyone at the Bible school in Nagabagre. Kabore had been praying that he too might be Spirit baptized and empowered for ministry in signs and wonders before graduation. And at a quarter past two in the morning, he began singing in tongues, and with his leather lungs, he didn't need a microphone. Everyone woke up—missionaries, national pastors, and students—and went to the chapel.

The meeting continued for three months, twenty-four hours a day. At the end of those ninety days, twenty-five hundred people had been baptized in the Spirit and thirty-five hundred won to

Christ by those newly Spirit-filled believers. Even Muslims, drawn to the chapel by loud praying, soon found themselves unable to stand on their feet because of God's mighty power. Fearing for their lives and prostrate on the floor, they asked Christians praying nearby, "What is this?" To which the Christians responded, "It is the power of Jesus." "But we don't believe in Jesus as Savior," the Muslims answered. "Do you believe in Him now?" the Christians would ask. "Yes, we must believe or die in our sins." Within a few minutes of confessing the Lordship of Christ, they would begin speaking in tongues, having been baptized in the Holy Spirit.

This revival has continued. From fifteen thousand members, the church has grown to over four hundred thousand, and runs on the wheels of a hundred thousand women who fast and pray every Monday. At this rate, a million people—one of every eight in Burkina Faso—will know Jesus Christ by the year 2000. Significantly, the focus has been less on tongues than on holiness, dealing with sin in Christ's body...Aspects of the revival convinced me that some of Satan's territories cannot be penetrated without the power of the Holy Spirit in signs and wonders.[1]

This above report is one of many accounts of God's visitations across our planet in the last several years. Stories of such revivals have come from Argentina, Brazil, Chili, Cuba, China and many countries in Africa. I am convinced that the Spirit desires to invade America, Canada, Europe and England with this same demonstration of His grace, goodness and greatness. Our world and the Church are in desperate need of moral holiness, spiritual transformation and Spirit-empowered living that only the Word of God can deliver. But, I believe it will require the same cost of desperation that takes us back to a simple confidence in God's Word and God's Spirit to work in our midst. It is my contention that the best place and time for the Spirit to engage us is when we gather to hear from God's Word and to genuinely expect His miraculous wonders. So my concluding words are words of challenge found in this title, *Speak the Word, Expect the Wonder!*

REFERENCES

CHAPTER ONE REFERENCES

1. Stenger, Victor J. *God the Failed Hypothesis* (Amherst, N Y.: Prometheus Books, 2007), 45.

2. Ibid. 11.

3. Kaiser, Walter C. Jr. *Toward an Exegetical Theology* (Grand Rapids, Mi.: Baker House, 2006), 22.

4. Vines, Jerry. *A Guide to Effective Sermon Delivery* (Chicago, Il.: Moody Press, 1986), 147.

5. Quicke, Michael J. *360-Degree Preaching* (Grand Rapids, Mi.: Baker Academic, 2006), 33.

6. Fee, Gordon D. *God's Empowering Presence* (Peabody, Ma.: Hendrickson Publishers, Inc., 1994), 848.

7. Crabtree, Charles T. *The Pentecostal Pulpit* (Springfield, Mo.: Gospel Publishing House, 2003), 28.

8. Ravenhill, David. *They Drank From the River and Died In the Wilderness* (Shippensburg, Pa.: Destiny Image Publishers, 2000), 72.

9. Ross, Hugh. *Why the Universe Is The Way It Is* (Grand Rapids, Mi.: Baker Books, 2008), 103.

10. Ibid. 104.

11. Ibid. 108.

12. Zacharias, Ravi. *The End of Reason* (Grand Rapids, Mi.: Zondervan Press, 2008), 17.

13. Ibid. 22.

14. Ibid. 117.

15. DeArteaga, William. *Quenching the Spirit* (Lake Mary, Fl.: Creation House, 1992), 16.

16. Ibid. 16.

CHAPTER TWO REFERENCES

1. Mounce, William D., Gen. Ed. *Mounce's Complete Expository Dictionary of Old & New Testament Words* (Grand Rapids, Mi.: Zondervan Press, 2006), 212.

2. Glynn, Patrick. *God The Evidence* (Rocklin, Ca.: Prima Publishing, 1007), 32.

3. Quicke, Michael J., *360-Degree Preaching* (Grand Rapids: Baker Academic, 2003), 27.

4. Ibid. 42.

5. Bloesch, Donald G., *A Theology of Word & Spirit* (Downers Grove: InterVarsity Press, 1992), 221.

6. Ibid. 137.

7. Ogilve, Lloyd J. "Preaching to the Powerful," Michael Duduit, Ed. *Preaching with Power* (Grand Rapids: Baker Books, 2006), 150.

8. Jakes, T. D. "Preaching to Mend Broken Lives," Michael Duduit, Ed. *Preaching with Power* (Grand Rapids: Baker Books, 2006), 69.

9. Ibid. 71.

10. Ibid. 73.

11. Harris, Ralph W. *Acts Today* (Springfield, Mo.: Gospel Publishing House, 1995), 43.

12. Franqipane, Francis. *The House of The Lord* (Lake Mary, Fl.: Creation House, 1991), 29.

13. Fee, Gordon D. *Listening To The Spirit in The Text* (Grand Rapids, Mi.: William B. Eerdmans Publishing, 2000), 7.

14. Ibid. 14.

15. Anderson, Leith. *A Church for the 21st. Century* (Minneapolis, Mn.: Bethany House, 1992), 21.

16. Ibid. 62.

17. Hesselgrave, David J. *Communicating Christ Cross-Culturally* (Grand Rapids, Mi.: Zondervan Publishing House, 1991), 25.

CHAPTER THREE REFERENCES

1. Bloesch, Donald G., *A Theology of Word & Spirit* (Downers Grove: InterVarsity Press, 1992), 220.

2. Ibid. 222.

3. Ibid. 223.

4. Ibid. 224.

5. Grant, Peter J., "The Priority of Apologetics in the Church," Ravi Zacharias and Norman Geisler, Eds. *Is Your Church Ready?* (Grand Rapids: Zondervan, 2003), 70.

6. Ibid. 66

7. Guest, John, "The Church as the Heart and Soul of Apologetics," Ravi Zacharias and Norman Geisler Eds. *Is Your Church Ready?* (Grand Rapids: Zondervan, 2003), 40.

8. Ibid. 54.

9. Ireland, David, *Activating the Gifts of the Holy Spirit,* (New Kensington, Pa: Whitaker House, 1997), 10.

10. Hughes, Ray H. *Pentecostal Preaching* (Cleveland, Tn.: Pathway Press, 1981), 12.

11. Ibid. 28.

12. Ibid. 33.

13. Ibid. 68-69.

14. Ibid. 108.

15. Ibid. 136-137.

16. Kraft, Charles H. *I Give You Authority* (Grand Rapids, Mi.: Chosen Books, 1997), 154.

CHAPTER FOUR REFERENCES

1. Bruce, F. F. *Tyndale New Testament* Commentaries, *the Letter Of Paul To The Romans* (Grand Rapids: William B. Eerdmans Publishing Company, 1987), 141.

2. Ibid. 143.

3. Ibid. 147.

4. Ibid. 149.

5. Ibid. 153.

6. Dunn, James, D. G. *Jesus and the Spirit*, (Grand Rapids: William B. Eerdmans Publishing, 1997), 310.

7. Ibid. 311.

8. Ibid. 312.

9. Ibid. 336.

10. Ibid. 338.

11. Nori, Don. *His Manifest Presence*, (Shippensburg, Pa: Destiny Image Publishing, 1992), 123.

12. Ibid. 123.

13. Crabtree, Charles T. *Pentecostal Preaching*, (Springfield, Mo: Gospel Publishing House, 2003), 9.

14. Green, Michael. *Evangelism in the Early Church* (Grand Rapids, Mi.: William b. Eerdmans Publishing, 1991), 148.

15. Ibid. 202-203.

CHAPTER FIVE REFERENCES

1. Barclay, William. *The Gospel of Matthew* Volume 1 (Louisville, Ky.: Westminster John Knox Press, 2001), 57.

2. Tenney, Merrill C. *John: The Gospel of Belief* (Grand Rapids, Mi.: William B. Eerdmans Publishing, 1997), 307.

3. Dunn, James D. G. *Jesus and The Spirit* (Grand Rapids,Mi.: William B. Eerdmans Publishing, 1997), 48.

4. Ibid. 49.

5. Gangel, Kenneth O. "Acts." in the Holman New Testament Commentary Series, Max Anders, Gen. Ed. (Nashville, Tn.: Broadman &Holman Publishers, 1998), 31.

6. Dunn, 262.

7. Ibid. 265.

8. Ibid. 310.

9. Ibid. 155.

10. Fee, Gordon D. *Gospel and Spirit* (Peabody, Mass.: Hendrickson Publishers, Inc., 1991), 44.

11. Ibid. 98.

12. Ibid. 111.

13. Aker, Benny C. and McGee, Gary B. Eds. *Signs & Wonders* (Springfield, Mo.: Gospel Publishing House, 1996), 34-35.

14. Menzies, William W. and Robert P. *Spirit and Power* (Grand Rapids, Mi.: Zondervan Publishing House, 2000), 150-151.

15. Ervin, Howard M. *Spirit Baptism* (Peabody, Ma.: Hendrickson Publishing, 1987), 6.

16. Ibid. 177.

CHAPTER SIX REFERENCES

1. Fee, Gordon D. *Gospel and Spirit* (Peabody, Ma.: Hendrickson, 1991), 111.

2. Ibid. 114.

3. Ibid. 115.

4. Ibid. 115.

5. Ibid. 102.

6. Pinnock, Clark H. *Flame of Love* (Downers Grove, Il.: InterVarsity Press, 1996), 11.

7. Ibid. 12.

8. Ibid. 91.

9. Ibid. 119.

10. Ibid. 163.

11. Pickett, Fuchsia. *The Next Move Of God* (Orlando, Fl.: Creation House, 1994), 10.

12. Ibid. 11.

13. Vines, Jerry. *A Guide To Effective Sermon Delivery* (Chicago, Il.: Moody Press, 1086), 160.

14. Ibid. 70.

15. Carlson, G. Raymond. *Spiritual Dynamics* (Springfield, Mo.: Gospel Publishing House, 1976), 22.

CHAPTER SEVEN REFERENCES

1. Bruce, F.F. *The Book of the Acts* (Grand Rapids, Mi.: William B. Eerdmans Publishing Company, 1988), 36.

2. Ibid. 36.

3. Ibid. 61.

4. Wood, George O. *Acts: The Holy Spirit at Work in Believers* (Springfield, Mo.: Global University, 2006), 63.

5. Ibid. 63.

6. Ibid. 78.

7. Menzies, William W. and Robert P. *Spirit and Power* (Grand Rapids, Mi.: Zondervan Publishing House, 2000), 152.

8. Ibid. 152.

9. Johnson, Bill. *The Supernatural Power of a Transformed Mind* (Shippensburg, Pa.: Destiny Image Publishers, 2005), 156.

10. Freidon, Claudio. *Holy Spirit, I Hunger for You* (Orlando, Fl.: Creation House, 1997), 16.

11. Dunnam, Maxie, "Power for Christian Living." John N. Akers, John H. Armstrong, and John D. Woodbridge, Eds. *This We Believe* (Grand Rapids, Mi.: Zondervan Publishing House, 2000), 141.

12. Ireland, David. *Activating the Gifts of the Holy Spirit* (New Kensington, Pa.: Whitaker House, 1997), 111.

CHAPTER EIGHT REFERENCES

1. Barclay, William. *The* Gospel *of Matthew Volume I* (Louisville, Ky.: Westminster John Knox Press, 2001), 54.

2. McGhee, Quentin. *The Life and Teachings of Christ* (Irving Tx.: ICI University Press, 1998), 40.

3. Bruce, F. F. *The Hard Sayings of Jesus* (Downers Grove, Il.: InterVarsity Press, 1983), 123.

4. Ibid. 122.

5. Ibid. 124.

6. Wright, John W. *Telling God's Story* (Downers Grove, Il.: Inter Varsity Press, 2007), 24.

7. Ibid. 25.

8. Freidzon, Claudio. *Holy Spirit, I Hunger for You* (Orlando, Fl.: Creation House, 1997), 128.

9. Ibid. 46.

10. Ibid. 57-58.

11. Medefind, Jedd and Lokkesmoe, Eric. *The Revolutionary Communicator* (Orlando, Fl.: Relevant Media Group, 2004), 72.

12. Van Der Elst, Dirk. *Culture As Given, Culture As Choice* (Prospect Heights, Il.: Waveland Press, 2003), 15.

13. Niles, D. T. "The Work of the Holy Spirit in the World". Gerald H. Anderson, Ed. *Christian Mission in Theological Perspective* (Nashville, Tn.: Abingdon Press, 1967), 93.

14. Rutz, James. *Mega Shift* (Colorado Springs, Co.: Empowerment Press, 2005), 16.

15. McPherson, Aimee Semple. *The Four-Square Gospel* (Los Angeles, Ca.: Foursquare Publications, 1969), 135.

16. Cox, Harvey. *Fire From Heaven* (Cambridge, Ma.: Da Capo Press, 1995), 110.

CHAPTER NINE REFERENCES

1. Barclay, William. *The Gospel of Matthew Volume I* (Louisville, Ky.: Westminster John Knox Press, 2001), 54.

2. McGhee, Quentin. *The Life and Teachings of Christ* (Irving Tx.: ICI University Press, 1998), 40.

3. Bruce, F. F. *The Hard Sayings of Jesus* (Downers Grove, Il.: InterVarsity Press, 1983), 123.

4. Ibid. 122.

5. Ibid. 124.

6. Wright, John W. *Telling God's Story* (Downers Grove, Il.: Inter Varsity Press, 2007), 24.

7. Ibid. 25.

8. Freidzon, Claudio. *Holy Spirit, I Hunger for You* (Orlando, Fl.: Creation House, 1997), 128.

9. Ibid. 46.

10. Ibid. 57-58.

11. Medefind, Jedd and Lokkesmoe, Eric. *The Revolutionary Communicator* (Orlando, Fl.: Relevant Media Group, 2004), 72.

12. Van Der Elst, Dirk. *Culture As Given, Culture As Choice* (Prospect Heights, Il.: Waveland Press, 2003), 15.

13. Niles, D. T. "The Work of the Holy Spirit in the World". Gerald H. Anderson, Ed. *Christian Mission in Theological Perspective* (Nashville, Tn.: Abingdon Press, 1967), 93.

14. Rutz, James. *Mega Shift* (Colorado Springs, Co.: Empowerment Press, 2005), 16.

15. McPherson, Aimee Semple. *The Four-Square Gospel* (Los Angeles, Ca.: Foursquare Publications, 1969), 135.

16. Cox, Harvey. *Fire From Heaven* (Cambridge, Ma.: Da Capo Press, 1995), 110.

CONCLUSION REFERENCES

1. Tarr, Dell "The Church and The Spirit's Power" Benny C. Aker & Gary B. McGee, Eds. *Signs & Wonders in Ministry Today* (Springfield, Mo.: Gospel Publishing House, 1996), 9-10.

CPSIA information can be obtained at www.ICGtesting.com
Printed in the USA
BVOW030759090812

297432BV00002B/7/P